THE OBELISKS OF EGYPT

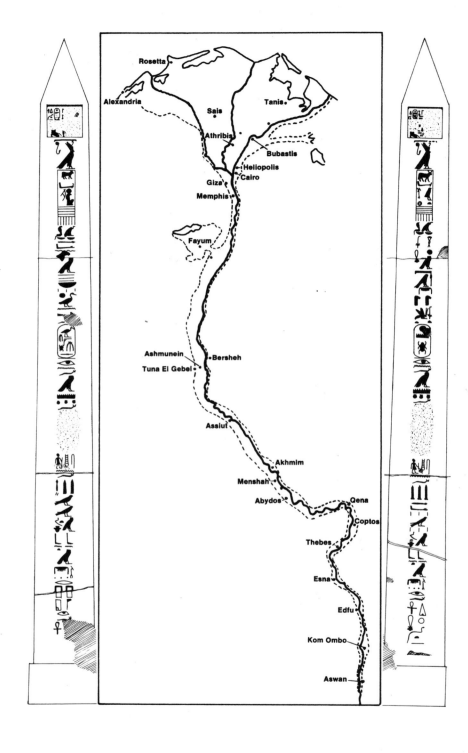

THE OBELISKS
OF EGYPT

SKYSCRAPERS OF THE PAST

LABIB HABACHI

EDITED BY

Charles C. Van Siclen III

J. M. DENT & SONS LTD

London   Toronto   Melbourne

© Charles Scribner's Sons 1977
First published in Great Britain 1978
All rights reserved
Made in Great Britain by
Biddles Ltd, Guildford
for
J. M. Dent & Sons Ltd
Aldine House, Albemarle Street, London

British Library Cataloguing in Publication Data

Habachi, Labib
    The obelisks of Egypt.
    1. Obelisks
    I. Title
    932   DT62.02

    ISBN 0-460-12045-X

Frontispiece. Map of Egypt, showing sites mentioned in this book, flanked
on each side by an obelisk of Tuthmosis III

To my wife Attiya,
in gratitude and affection

CONTENTS

ILLUSTRATIONS

FIGURES

PREFACE

LITTLE remains of the triumphs of the ancient Egyptians, but their obelisks still bear witness to their former skill, might, and piety. The accomplishments of long ago outshone those of more recent times, for the Egyptians succeeded, with often primitive methods, in extracting, moving over land and water, adorning, and erecting the great monolithic obelisks more than thirty-eight centuries ago. Inscribed with the names of their makers and of the gods they worshiped, the golden-tipped obelisks pierced the skies over ancient cities: Thebes, Memphis, Heliopolis, Piramesse. They remain mute symbols of the long-lost glory of ancient Egypt.

Whether they are still standing in their original places in Egypt or adorning a square or park in another country, obelisks always attract attention by their polish, their decoration, and above all their lofty height. In more than one text, the pharaohs boasted that the obelisks they erected reached, pierced, or mingled with the sky—in a way describing them as "skyscrapers." It is not without justification that I call them the skyscrapers of the past.

The gigantic Unfinished Obelisk, still lying in its quarry in Aswan in southern Egypt, has been an object of admiration for all who have seen it. Its enormous size and the remarkable, if rather primitive, method used to shape it never fail to provoke astonishment. In Luxor, three large obelisks still on their original sites stand among extensive ruins as imposing monuments to the engineering and artistic skills of the ancient Egyptians.

Some fifty years ago I was in charge of the Aswan Inspectorship of Antiquities, then covering an area from Abu Simbel in the south almost to the site of ancient Thebes (modern Luxor) in the north. Within this area, which extends along the Nile for more than three hundred miles, all the obelisks described in this book—and others—were quarried. But my real interest in these obelisks began only about twenty-five years ago, when I began a study of certain inscriptions in that region, inscriptions which were then hardly known. These related to obelisks quarried there, and most were carved by people who had been connected in some way with the production of obelisks.

I welcome the opportunity of writing about these splendid monuments. Although many books on the subject have already been published, most of them were written long ago, and many are out of date or are unavailable to those who are interested in the history and purpose of obelisks. Recently, some excellent books have been written on the obelisks of Rome and other cities, but these are concerned primarily with their history at their present sites.

This book does not claim to discuss all obelisks; small ones without important inscriptions have been omitted. The inscriptions on obelisks usually include all the names of the king responsible for their erection, and these are replete with pompous phrases about the royal power and about royal devotion to the country and to the solar deities. In the examples of the inscriptions included here, the emphasis is placed upon the sections which bear on the history and religion of Egypt. From these, I hope my readers will gain a clearer understanding of the nature of obelisks.

The book is divided into seven chapters. The first is devoted to the religious and historical importance of obelisks in general. The second deals with the way these monuments were produced and erected. The next three discuss chronologically the obelisks at Heliopolis and Memphis, in the Theban area, and at Piramesse and other places that have a connection with the solar gods. The sixth chapter discusses the obelisks in Rome and the one in Istanbul, all of which were removed from Egypt in the first centuries of the present era. The final chapter is concerned with the obelisks which were taken from Egypt to Paris, London, and New York in the nineteenth century.

In writing this book, I have been helped by a number of colleagues and friends. I must mention in particular George R. Hughes, John A. Wilson, David O'Connor, and Rowland Ellis, all of whom were kind enough to look through the manuscript and make useful suggestions. I have to thank especially Charles C. Van Siclen III, who made my book easy to read and better documented. My thanks are also due to Dr. Gamal Mukhtar, undersecretary of state in the Ministry of Culture and president of the Egyptian Antiquities Organization and of the Egyptian Center of Documentation; to the Franco-Egyptian Center at Karnak, and particularly its head, Jean Lauffray, and one of its artists, Claudine Gueniot. I am grateful to my friends Joseph Farber, Jim Dalmage, Max Hirmer, Bruce Hungerford, John Ross, George Bourdelon, and Harry James for supplying some of the illustrations included here. I also wish to thank Charles Francis Nims for allowing me to stay at Chicago House in Luxor; I have profited from his extensive knowledge of the Theban area. Thanks too go to Roland and Lydia Redmond, who guided me through the crowded streets of Rome, and to Froelich Rainey and his assistants in the University Museum, Philadelphia, for helping me in the completion of the manuscript. Last but not least, I must thank Walter A. Fairservis, Jr., Kenneth Heuer, and my wife Attiya, all of whom encouraged me to write my first and perhaps my only popular book and maintained their interest over the seven years during which I worked on it. I hope that, in spite of the long delay, it is worthy of the subject it treats.

LABIB HABACHI

THE OBELISKS OF EGYPT

CHAPTER ONE

The Meaning of Obelisks

AMONG remains of the great civilizations of the past, Mesopotamian, Egyptian, Greek, or Roman, the obelisks of Egypt are undoubtedly more often seen and better known than any other monuments. Some of the smaller obelisks and fragments of larger ones are familiar to the numerous visitors of museums in various countries; larger ones which are still on their original sites are admired by the thousands of people who visit Egypt each year. Still others are seen by the crowds who pass through London, Paris, New York, Istanbul, and especially Rome, where there are more obelisks than in any other place.

An obelisk is a four-sided single piece of stone standing upright, gradually tapering as it rises and terminating in a small pyramid called a "pyramidion." Obelisks were known to the ancient Egyptians as *Tekhenu*, a word whose derivation is unknown. When the Greeks became interested in Egypt, both obelisks and pyramids attracted their attention. To the former they gave the name *"obeliskos,"* from which the modern name in almost all languages is derived. *Obeliskos* is a Greek diminutive meaning "small spit"; it was applied to obelisks because of their tall, narrow shape. In Arabic, the term is *Messalah,* which means a large patching needle and again has reference to the object's form.

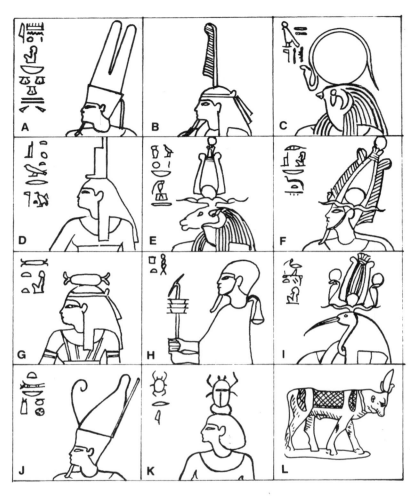

FIGURE 1. Gods of Egypt associated with obelisks: (A) Amun-Re, (B) Shu (C) Re-Harakhti, (D) Isis, (E) Khnum, (F) Osiris, (G) Neit, (H) Ptah, (I) Thoth, (J) Atum, (K) Kheperi, (L) Mnevis

Obelisks were considered by the ancient Egyptians to be sacred to the sun god,[1] whose main center of worship was at Heliopolis, the ruins of which lie in the district of Matariya near Cairo. Although the well-known obelisks date from the twentieth century B.C., such monuments seem to have been erected there in honor of the sun god in much earlier periods.

A type of stone resembling the pyramidion of an obelisk was

apparently considered sacred to the sun god even before the appearance of the first pharaoh in the First Dynasty (c. 3100–2890 B.C.). Such stones, known as *ben* or *benben*, were believed to have existed in Heliopolis from time immemorial and were the fetish of the primeval god Atum (the setting sun) (fig. 1J) and the god Re or Re-Harakhti (the rising sun) (fig. 1C). The stones were also associated with the *Benu*-bird, or phoenix (plate 1). This creature, which begot itself, was thought to have come from the east to live in Heliopolis for five hundred years and then to return to the east to be buried by the young phoenix which would in turn replace it in Heliopolis. According to one version of the tale, instead of being replaced the bird revived itself, and thus it was connected with the god of the dead. In some tombs, an image of the phoenix is shown among the gods.

In the pyramids of the last king of the Fifth Dynasty and the kings of the Sixth Dynasty (c. 2345–2181 B.C.), the walls of the burial chamber were decorated with Pyramid Texts, religious texts concerned with the welfare of the deceased. One text reads: "O Atum, the Creator. You became high on the height, you rose up as the *benben*-stone in the mansion of the 'Phoenix' in Heliopolis." [2] Pliny the Elder (A.D. 23–79), the Roman encyclopedist, wrote that obelisks were meant to resemble the rays of the sun.[3] This comparison finds support in an inscription addressed to the sun god: *"Ubenek em Benben"* ["You shine in the *benben*-stone."].[4] During the prosperous days of the Eighteenth Dynasty (1570–1320 B.C.), and perhaps at other times, the pyramidions of obelisks were covered with gold or some other metal. The date at which obelisks were first erected is not known, but the kings of the Fifth Dynasty (2494–2345 B.C.), who were fervent worshipers of the sun god, may have been the earliest rulers to decorate the façades of their temples with pairs of such monuments.

Heliopolis, the city of the sun, was called by the ancient Egyptians *Iunu*, a name meaning "the pillar," and sometimes *Iunu Meht*, "the northern pillar." The name *Iunu* appears in the Bible as *n*; Heliopolis is the Greek name by which the city is generally known. Heliopolis was sacred to the sun god Re and his ennead, a group of nine associated gods. Other gods worshiped there included Kheperi (fig. 1K), the scarab, and Shu (fig. 1B), the god of the air. Obelisks were first erected at Heliopolis and the practice was continued throughout the pharaonic period. The majority of these obelisks have been removed or destroyed; the only one still standing there is that of Sesostris I (1971–1928 B.C.).

Ancient Thebes (modern Luxor) was known as *Uast*, "the scepter," or sometimes as *Iunu Shemayit*, "the southern pillar," or as "the Heliopolis of the south." Its main god, Amun, was represented in human form with a crown of tall feathers. He was later assimilated with Re and was known as Amun-Re (fig. 1A), "King of the Gods." Because of this identification, obelisks were raised on his behalf. In Thebes, the center of his cult, numerous obelisks, including many of the largest, were erected in honor of Amun-Re, at the time when the city was the capital of Egypt. Of its obelisks, only three survive; some were destroyed and a few were taken abroad.

Piramesse—that is, *Per-Ramessu*, "the domain of Ramesses"— became the capital of Egypt in the reign of Ramesses II (1304–1237 B.C.) and remained so under the succeeding Ramesside kings of the nineteenth and twentieth dynasties (1320–1200 and 1200–1085 B.C.). It was embellished with a score of obelisks, for the most part fashioned by Ramesses II, although several made by earlier kings were taken over by him. Most of these obelisks were smaller than those of Thebes. The cults of the great gods, Re, Amun-Re, and Ptah of Memphis (fig. 1H), were introduced in the new capital, and the names of these and other gods appear upon the obelisks Ramesses II erected there.

Elsewhere, only rather small obelisks have been found. The inscriptions on these make it clear that they were erected in honor of local divinities who were either solar gods or associated with the solar cult. Two pairs of obelisks which were recovered from the ruins on the island of Elephantine near Aswan were dedicated to Khnum (fig. 1E), the ram-headed god who fashioned mankind upon a potter's wheel. He was later associated with the sun god Re and was known as Khnum-Re. His obelisks were set up at the "altar of Re"—probably in a solar chapel. During the nineteenth century a pair of Ptolemaic obelisks dedicated to Isis (fig. 1D) was unearthed on the island of Philae. On them are mentioned the solar gods Atum and Amun-Re. At Abu Simbel, a chapel of Re-Harakhti adjacent to the Great Temple of Ramesses II, contained a pair of obelisks and other cult objects related to the sun god.

An obelisk found at Minshah in Middle Egypt undoubtedly once stood at the neighboring religious center of Abydos. On this obelisk the king is called "beloved of Osiris" (fig. 1F), the god of the dead, who was the principal god of Abydos, although other deities also had cult places there. There were once

PLATE 1. The Egyptian phoenix standing behind the figure of the goddess Nephthys in the guise of a falcon, from the tomb of Queen Nefertari, wife of Ramesses II

two obelisks in Ashmunein, also in Middle Egypt, both dedicated to Thoth (fig. 1I), god of writing and wisdom, and titulary deity of the place. Among Thoth's many attributes was that of "representative of Re." The ibis and the baboon were sacred to Thoth, and the latter animals were often shown adoring the sun god. In the quarries of Gebel el-Ahmar near Cairo an obelisk is depicted standing between two baboons with their front legs raised in worship (fig. 2).[5]

An inscription on a fragment of an obelisk from Horbeit in the eastern part of the Delta mentions Osiris and his sacred bull, the Mnevis (fig. 1L), known as "the living soul of Re." At Athribis in the center of the Delta the pedestals and a few fragments of the shafts of two obelisks still remain. On one fragment, the king is shown with local divinities, one of which is Atum. A number of obelisks were also raised in honor of Atum, a local god of Sais, which was a political center in the Delta and capital of the country during the Saite Period (664–525 B.C.).

The kings who erected obelisks were usually described on them as beloved of various local and solar gods, and in many cases the king was shown in close relationship to these divinities. One text from an obelisk describes the king as "appearing like Harakhti, beautiful as King of the Two Lands like Atum," and a second, as "the one whom Atum made to be King of the Two Lands and to whom [he] gave Egypt, the desert, and foreign lands."

On some obelisks there are references to royal victories, but these are rarely actual historical events. The boasts on most of the obelisks erected by Ramesses II are particularly suspect. On one, this king is commemorated as "the one who defeats the land of Asia, who vanquishes the Nine Bows, who makes the foreign lands as if they were not." On another it is said, "His power is like that of Monthu [the god of war], the bull who tramples the foreign lands and kills the rebels." The king is described as recipient of tribute, noble governor, brave, and vigilant.

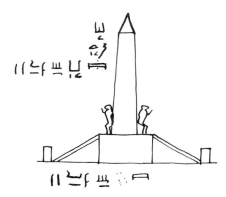

FIGURE 2. Baboons adoring an obelisk

If the claims of Ramesses II are not justified, those of his predecessor Tuthmosis III carry greater weight. In celebration of the great victory which Tuthmosis III gained over his powerful enemies in Asia, he erected two obelisks at the Temple of Karnak; the upper part of one of these survives in Istanbul. On one side of it, the king is spoken of as "the lord of victory, who subdues every [land] and who establishes his frontier at the beginning of the earth [the extreme south] and at the marshland up to Naharina [in the north]." On another side, he is said to have crossed the Euphrates with his army to make great slaughter. This crossing of the river was a great achievement, equaled only by his grandfather Tuthmosis I. It provided sufficient justification for the erection of the obelisks.

Yet another reason for setting up obelisks is indicated on the Istanbul obelisk, where Tuthmosis III is described as "a king who conquers all the lands, long of life and lord of Jubilees." Beginning in the thirtieth year of a king's reign, and every three years thereafter, a festival of renewal was celebrated. On the occasion of these jubilees, the kings set up obelisks. The obelisk of Queen Hatshepsut (1503–1482 B.C.), which still stands at the Temple of Karnak, describes her as "the one for whom her father Amun established the name 'Makare' upon the *Ashed*-tree [a tree of eternity] in reward for this hard, beautiful, and excellent monument which she made for her First Jubilee." However, since Hatshepsut reigned about twenty years, she evidently celebrated her Jubilee much earlier.

FIGURE 3. Scarab

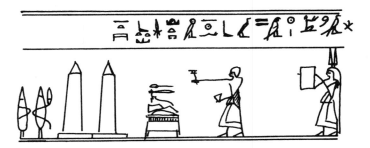

FIGURE 4. Vignette from the *Book of the Dead*

Obelisks were always regarded by the ancient Egyptians as a symbol of the sun god related to the *Benben,* but during certain periods they were looked upon as being themselves occupied by a god and thus entitled to offerings. This is the case with four obelisks erected by Tuthmosis III in the Temple of Amun-Re at Karnak. In an inscription there, the king recorded the establishment of new feasts and offerings which he instituted for the four obelisks, dedicating twenty-five loaves of bread and a jar of beer to each of them daily. When an obelisk was erected, scarabs (fig. 3) showing the king kneeling in adoration before it were issued.[6] A vignette (fig. 4) accompanying the fifteenth chapter of the *Book of the Dead,* a guide to the dead in their travels through the Underworld, is entitled "Adoring Re-Harakhti when he rises in the eastern horizon of the sky." In the scene are two priests, one reciting from a roll of papyrus which he holds, the other making offerings to two obelisks which embody Re-Harakhti.

The positioning of obelisks followed a regular pattern. Ramesses II gave names to the pair of obelisks which he erected before the pylon of the Luxor Temple. On the pedestal of the eastern obelisk, which is still *in situ*, the king boasted that "he made a large obelisk [called] Ramesses-Beloved-of-Amun [the rising sun]." The western obelisk, which is now in Paris, was named "Ramesses-Beloved-of-Atum [the setting sun]." On the eastern obelisk the king is called "beloved of Harakhti [the rising sun]," while on the western one he is styled "beloved of Atum." The names of each obelisk and the epithets on them correspond to the rising of the sun in the east and its setting in the west. Tuthmosis III erected two obelisks in Heliopolis, one of which is now in New York and the other in London. The New York obelisk mentions Harakhti while the London one refers to Atum. Based on the parallel provided by the position of the Luxor obelisk, it is evident that the obelisk of Tuthmosis III now in New York once stood at the east of the entrance of the temple in Heliopolis, while the one in London originally stood at the west.

The proper orientation of the faces of any obelisk can be found in the direction faced by the hieroglyphs which make up the inscriptions upon them (fig. 5). Hieroglyphic inscriptions,

FIGURE 5. Direction of inscriptions on obelisks

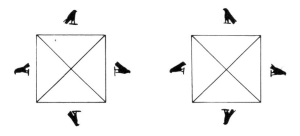

whether written in horizontal lines or vertical columns, can be read either from left to right or from right to left, but the hieroglyphs normally face toward the beginning of the inscription. The hieroglyphs on the front of the obelisk, which usually has a dedicatory inscription, and those on the back both face toward the entranceway of the temple. Those on the sides of the obelisk face toward the front of the temple. For any individual obelisk there can be but one correct orientation on either side of the entrance of the temple.[7]

In addition to large obelisks as an emblem or symbol of the sun god, smaller obelisks—or rather obeliskoid objects—were sometimes placed in front of tombs. These objects were inscribed on only one face with the name and the main title of the tomb owner, in the same manner as the name and titles carved on the lintel and jambs of some of the doors of the tombs of the Old Kingdom (2686–2181 B.C.). Some bear prayers addressed to the gods of the dead on behalf of the tomb owner. Most of these objects face east, and they may relate to the sun god who served as guide to the deceased in the Underworld.

During the Old Kingdom, the kings erected pyramids to serve as their burial places. In fact, the pyramids were but a focus of a large funerary complex with a mortuary temple at the base of the pyramid connected by means of a causeway to a valley temple on the edge of the cultivated area. The kings of the Fifth Dynasty, already mentioned as especially devoted to the sun god, added to their pyramid complexes solar temples in which a gigantic obelisk was the main feature.

In the interiors of several important tombs of the Eighteenth Dynasty were depicted scenes of the tomb owner's funeral procession advancing toward the Goddess of the West (fig. 6). A pair of obelisks being erected is usually shown in part of such scenes.[8] The materials of which these obelisks were formed are not definitely known, but most probably they too were stone. They seem to have been erected in honor of the sun god to secure the welfare of the deceased.

FIGURE 6. Funerary obelisk in the tomb of Rekhmire

Small obelisks, usually made of wood, were found in tombs along with boxes containing funerary figurines called *ushabti*. In order to release the deceased from obligatory work in the Afterworld, these ushabti were placed in the tomb to answer "Here I am" when the deceased was called to work. Obelisks were also pictured behind certain figures of the god Osiris in the tombs, which may help to explain their appearance in connection with the ushabti boxes.

While ancient Egyptians were the first people to fashion monuments in the form of obelisks, they seem to have influenced other peoples to produce or acquire such monuments. The Canaanites and the Phoenicians, through their contacts with the Egyptians during the Middle Kingdom (2050–1786 B.C.), came to erect small obelisks. The kings of Kush, residing south of Egypt at the Fourth Cataract of the Nile, built somewhat similar monuments for themselves. At one time their predecessors had ruled Egypt and had adopted the obelisk for their own use. In the middle of the seventh century B.C. the Assyrian king Assurbanipal sacked the ancient Egyptian city of Thebes. Among the items he reportedly carried off were two tall obelisks coated with bronze; no trace of these has ever come to light. In their turn, Roman emperors carried off obelisks to adorn Rome and Constantinople, and in the nineteenth century large Egyptian obelisks were acquired to adorn Paris, London, and New York.

The obelisk has been part of the architectural repertory of the Western world since classical times. Obelisks were inserted into architectural schemes in England and France. People used miniature obelisks as ornaments in their houses. Obelisks large and small were erected over private tombs; in Philadelphia, one of the wealthier citizens raised a large obelisk over his family burial vault. In Munich and Karlsruhe large obelisks were made locally to decorate the public squares. The largest obelisk, although not a true one since it is built of numerous blocks, is the Washington Monument in Washington, D.C. It is 169 meters (555 feet) high and has an observatory on the 500-foot level.[9]

CHAPTER TWO

How Obelisks Were Produced

OBELISKS are impressive not only for their lofty size and graceful form, but for their high polish and beautiful decoration. One cannot but marvel at the skill of the ancient Egyptians in producing such wonders with relatively primitive techniques.

Most obelisks, especially the larger ones, are made of granite, although a few are quartzite or basalt.[1] The Egyptian word for granite is *mat*, which means more specifically red granite. In conjunction with other words it can mean different types of granite; thus *mat en Abu* means "Elephantine granite"; *mat rudet*, "hard granite"; and *mat kemt*, "black granite." Quartzite, a compact form of sandstone, was called *bia* and basalt *bekhen*. Quartzite is found as a large deposit at Gebel el-Ahmar near Heliopolis, while basalt comes from the Wadi Hammamat in the Eastern Desert.

Granite, whether red or black, is found in Egypt only in the area around Aswan (fig. 7). It was quarried there in numerous places, but the most important quarries were those of the islands of Elephantine and Seheil, those near the Unfinished Obelisk south of Aswan, and those in Shellal opposite the island of Philae. There are also vast quarries of quartzite on the west bank of the Nile opposite Aswan, between the Monastery of

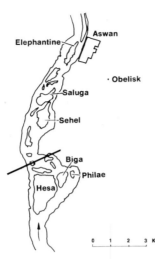

FIGURE 7. The Aswan region

St. Semeon and the tombs at Qubbet el-Hawa. Numerous large embankments lead down from these quarries to the river.

The huge Unfinished Obelisk at Aswan (plate 2) provides an opportunity to study the various stages of quarrying granite for the production of obelisks. The English archaeologist Reginald Engelbach (1888–1946), who worked for the Egyptian Department of Antiquities, wrote of it:

"A study of the Aswan [Unfinished] Obelisk enables the visitor to look with different eyes on the finished monuments, and to realise, not only the immense labour expended in transporting the giant blocks and the years of tedious extraction of stone in the quarries, but the heartbreaking failures which must sometimes have driven the old engineers to the verge of despair before a perfect monument could be presented by the king to his god. . . . A perfect monument teaches us little of their engineering; an imperfect or unfinished piece of work may teach us much. . . . The Aswan obelisk is a piece of work that failed, not through any fault of the workers, but owing to an unexpected fissure in the rock. It must have been galling beyond words to the Egyptians to abandon it after all the time and trouble they had expended, but today we are grateful for their failure, as it teaches us more about their methods than any monument in Egypt." [2]

The Unfinished Obelisk still lies in its quarry, detached on all but its lower side. If it had been extracted, it would have been 41.75 meters high with a base about 4.2 meters on each side. The total weight would have been 1168 tons, heavier than any piece of stone ever handled by the ancient Egyptians.

The selection of the proper section of the quarry from which to extract the large obelisk must have presented difficulties. Test shafts were sunk to determine the nature of the rock and to ensure that it was flawless. In this case, some of the test shafts seem to have been included in the trenches made to detach the obelisk on the north and the south. Work started by removing the uneven surface. This was accomplished by placing bricks upon the surface to be removed, heating them until they were quite hot, and then dousing them with cold water. The rock surface fractured and became easily detachable, rendering the surface reasonably smooth.

The detachment of the two sides of the obelisk was one of the most delicate stages of its removal. Large balls of dolerite, each weighing about 5.5 kilograms and measuring 15 to 30 centimeters, were found near the obelisk. Countless numbers of these had been brought from the valleys in the Eastern Desert where they occur naturally. The balls were apparently attached to rammers and were used by being struck vertically downward with great force. With regard to the trenches around the obelisk (plate 3), Engelbach wrote:

"We are struck with the absence of any marks of wedges or chisels. . . . The ancient chisels leave traces which are easily recognisable . . . but here we have the effect of a series of parallel, vertical 'cuts' just as if the rock had been extracted with a gigantic cheese-scoop. A further feature of the trench is that there are no corners—everything is rounded. . . . The only tools which could produce this effect are the dolerite balls. . . . The trench and pits were therefore not cut out, but rather bashed out." [3]

PLATE 2. The Unfinished Obelisk of Aswan, lying in its quarry

Several thousand men can be imagined arranged about the obelisk in groups of three, two standing, holding and raising the rammer, and the third squatting and directing the blow to its proper place. One man, or more, would sing or chant to maintain the rhythm of the blows and to divert the others during the long, hard work; such a scene is sometimes pictured in the ancient tombs. The same practice prevails today in building or digging operations, and especially in archaeological excavations: one man sings and the rest chant a phrase in response. With the use of the rammer, or *mindala,* as it is now called in Arabic, such songs as the following are heard:

CHORUS. *Ya Sayyid hizz el-hilal* (O Said, brandish the Crescent!)
SINGER. *M'Iskandaria li' sh-shellal* (From Alexandria to the Cataract)
CHORUS. *Ya Sayyid hizz el-hilal*
SINGER. *Duqqu ya awlad, khabar eih ummal* (Bash, boys! What's with you?)

When the songs are finished, the workmen repeat phrases such as *"Hela hop heila,"* the first two words being said as the rammer was raised and the third accompanying the down-

PLATE 3. Trenches around the Unfinished Obelisk, showing signs of its being quarried

stroke.[4] These words have no meaning in Arabic, and the workmen chant them without knowing their source. It is possible
that the words have come down from the ancient Egyptians.

How long the work on the Unfinished Obelisk (fig. 8) would
have taken cannot be determined accurately. On the base of an
obelisk still standing in Karnak, Queen Hatshepsut recorded that
the work on it was done in seven months from the time of quarrying. The queen in another place on the same shaft implored
the reader not to say, "It is a lie," and there is every reason to
accept her statement of the time involved. Engelbach considered
this a reasonable time for extracting the Unfinished Obelisk.[5]

Problems plagued the work. A fissure near the base of the
Unfinished Obelisk seems to have been discovered early; this
caused a reduction of about 8.4 meters in the projected height.
Other fissures began to appear, as indicated in fig. 8: a, b,
and c near the top and j, k, l, and m on the south side. These
necessitated still further reductions in the size of the obelisk.
The appearance of fissure p in the middle of the shaft finally
caused work to be suspended. After all the long and arduous
labor, this must have been a great blow not only to the
overseers but to the workmen as well. Even today the expert
workmen engaged to dig with archaeological expeditions take
great pride in their work; they often talk about it and tell how
they have been responsible for great discoveries.

Had the Unfinished Obelisk proved to be flawless, the lower
side would have been detached from the parent rock by pounding. Galleries would have been driven underneath and progres-
sively filled with planks of wood until the side was completely
detached. Work could have been done simultaneously from the
trenches on either side. In the same quarry there is an area
which seems originally to have been the bed of a small obelisk.
Here it is clear that the detachment from below was done by
pounding.

Holes for driving wedges are frequently met with in the
Aswan area, especially in the four quarrying areas from which
large monuments were removed. According to Engelbach, some

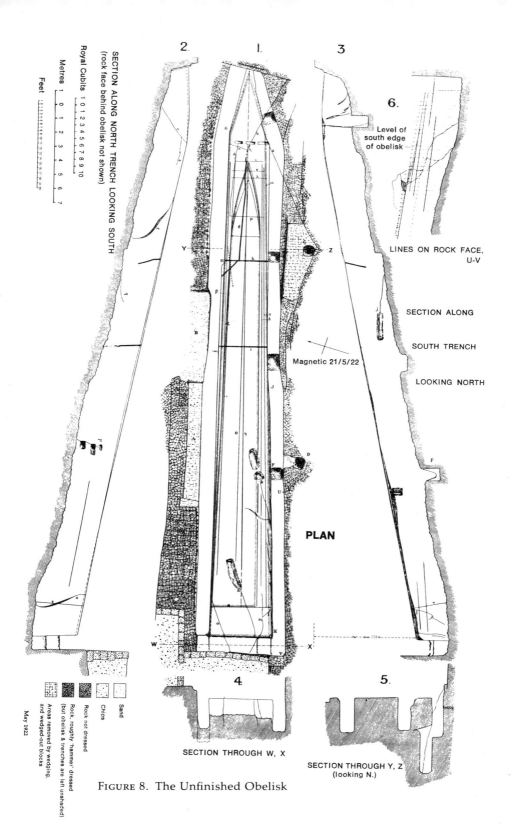

SECTION ALONG NORTH TRENCH LOOKING SOUTH
(rock face behind obelisk not shown)

Royal Cubits 10 1 2 3 4 5 6 7 8 9 10

Metres 1 0 1 2 3 4 5 6 7

Feet

2.

1.

3.

6.

Level of
south edge
of obelisk

LINES ON ROCK FACE,
U-V

SECTION ALONG

SOUTH TRENCH

LOOKING NORTH

Magnetic 21/5/22

Y

Z

W

X

PLAN

4.

5.

SECTION THROUGH W, X

SECTION THROUGH Y, Z
(looking N.)

Sand

Chips

Rock not dressed

Rock, roughly 'hammer' dressed
(but obelisk & trenches are left unshaded)

Areas removed by wedging,
and wedged-out blocks

May 1922

FIGURE 8. The Unfinished Obelisk

PLATE 4. The transport of the statue of Djehutihotep, reconstruction by Reginald Engelbach after a painting in his tomb at el-Bersheh

of these are modern, while others date to the period after the pharaohs. However, he believed that wedges were used by ancient Egyptians when necessary, although he could not accept the idea that wet wooden wedges were used to detach obelisks. Such wedges are more inclined to jump from their holes rather than to exert the proper pressure. Joseph Roeder, a German scholar, has recently suggested that only in Roman times were iron wedges used in detaching stone and iron chisels in dressing them; [6] in ancient Egypt pounding was the only method used to detach and dress blocks.

Once an obelisk was removed from the parent rock, work was begun to raise it from the quarry to an embankment on which it

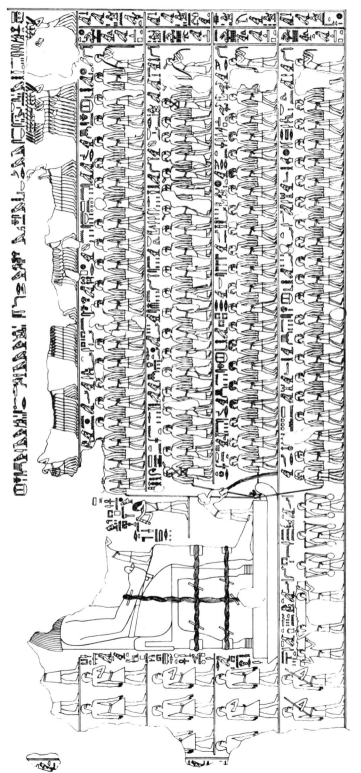

FIGURE 9. Transporting the statue of Djehutihotep, Bersheh

could be dragged down to the Nile. According to Engelbach, some thirty levers made from stout tree trunks had to be inserted in the trench around the obelisk with suitable packing. Handling ropes attached to the levers were used by several thousand men.

"By using these levers from both sides of the obelisk in turn, it could be made to rock slightly backwards and forwards and gradually be raised by increasing the height of the packing below at each heave. By this means, the base could be raised some 8 feet [2.43 meters] above its present level, and the quantity of rock to be removed from in front of the obelisk greatly reduced in consequence." [7]

When the obelisk had been raised high enough and a path cleared, it would be dragged down the slope to the river. Engelbach calculated that this could be done by 6,000 men pulling on 40 ropes, each 7.25 inches [18.4 cm.] in diameter.

At Bersheh opposite Ashmunein (near Mellawi in Middle Egypt), a governor of that district by the name of Djehutihotep (nineteenth century B.C.) had his tomb built. On its walls were depicted the transportation of a large seated statue of the owner, estimated to have been 60 tons in weight (fig. 9, plate 4). This statue is mounted on a sled pulled by 172 men, and a man pours a liquid before it to act as a lubricant. No rolers are seen under the sled. This had led some Egyptologists to believe that the ancient Egyptians did not use rollers, especially since no large ones have been discovered. Without such rollers, however, some 11,000 men would have been required to move the Unfinished Obelisk, and there is not sufficient space for so many. That the rollers have not survived is not surprising. Egypt is a country lacking in wood, and so valuable a commodity would not long have remained unused. [8]

Near the Unfinished Obelisk were found two wide embankments over which heavy blocks once had been pulled (fig. 10). Obelisks were supposedly pulled along the embankment indicated by the letters D–A, then along that marked F–E. Both embankments were still visible at the turn of the century but are

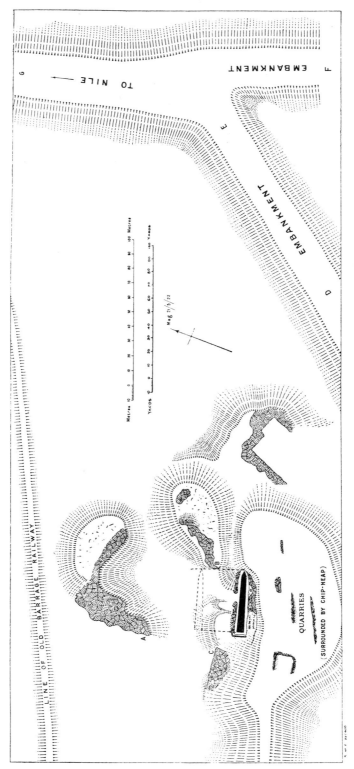

FIGURE 10. The Unfinished Obelisk and the embankments

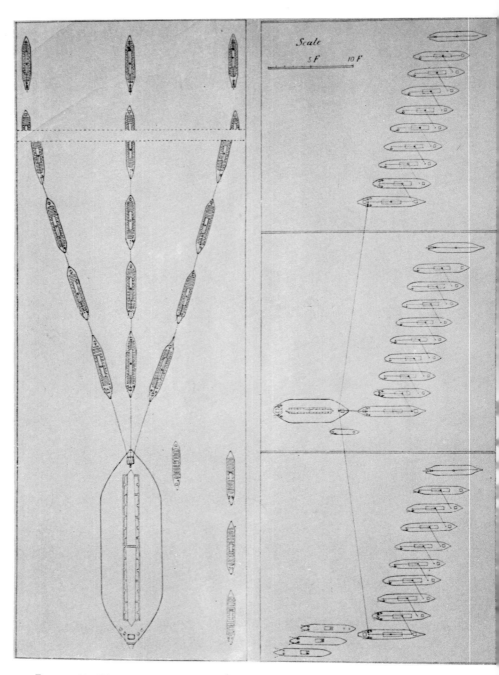

FIGURE 11. Plans of the ships towing an obelisk barge, two interpretations of
the Deir el-Bahari reliefs

hardly discernible today. The exact point at which the obelisks arrived at the river is not known; most probably it is covered by the modern town. No indication has been found to suggest how an obelisk could have been put on its barge. Again according to Engelbach, this could have been accomplished safely by bringing the barge as close as possible to the bank, building the embankment around and over it, pulling the obelisk directly over the barge, and letting it down into place by removing the fill around the barge. Once the barge was afloat the obelisk's journey to its destination would start.

Such journeys, usually undertaken during the annual flooding of the Nile, must have been pleasant. Queen Hatshepsut, in her funerary temple at Deir el-Bahari, west of Thebes, had pictured in a series of reliefs the journey of a pair of her obelisks from Elephantine to Thebes (fig. 11).[9] The two obelisks are shown end-to-end on a barge some 60.95 meters in length. The barge was towed by three rows of boats, nine in each row, with a tenth in the lead for the pilots. Accompanying the barge were three more boats in which religious ceremonies were performed. That great procession on the Nile must have been witnessed by thousands of people in the course of its journey.

When the obelisks finally arrived at Thebes, they must have been greeted with much ceremony. From Deir el-Bahari come scenes of soldiers running, holding aloft branches raised in greeting (fig. 12). Sacrifices were made and offerings presented to the gods. It was undoubtedly a great day for Hatshepsut and her courtiers and the citizens of Thebes. In an adjacent scene, the queen is shown presenting the obelisks to Amun-Re, king of the gods.

One most delicate operation still remained—the erection of the obelisks on their pedestals in the Temple of Karnak. A ramp of earth or sand had to be extended from the point of debarkation to the place where the obelisks were to stand. The obelisks were then dragged to that location and the task of erecting them begun. The opinions of engineers, architects, and archaeologists on how this was accomplished vary considerably, and a number

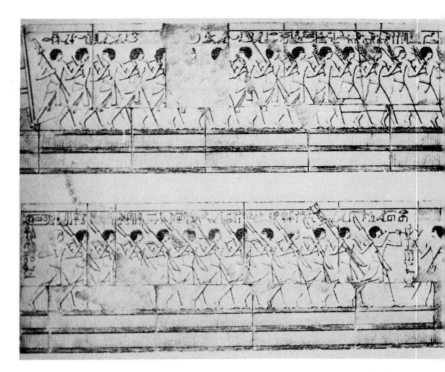

FIGURE 12. The reception of the obelisks of Hatshepsut, Deir el-Bahari

of different schemes have been suggested. The most significant are the hypothesis proposed by Engelbach and another, more recent one by the French archaeologist Henri Chevrier.

Having shown the difficulties encountered in erecting obelisks with the primitive means known to the ancient Egyptians, Engelbach suggested the following (plate 5):

"A method which is mechanically possible and which meets all observed facts is that the obelisk was not let down over the edge of an embankment, but down a funnel-shaped pit *in* the end of it, the lowering being done by removing sand, with which the pit had been filled, from galleries leading into the bottom of it, and so allowing the obelisk to settle slowly down. Taking this as the basis of the method, the form of the pit resolves itself into a tapering square-sectioned funnel—rather like a petrol-funnel—fairly wide at the top, but very little larger than the base of the obelisk at the bottom. The obelisk is in-

troduced into the funnel on a curved way leading gradually from the surface of the embankment until it engages smoothly with the hither wall of the funnel. The sand is removed by men with baskets through galleries leading from the bottom of the funnel to convenient places outside the embankment." [10]

Chevrier dismissed Engelbach's theory on the grounds that the obelisk could not stand being lowered into the funnel with the longer part unsupported in the air. There was a risk that the shaft would fracture since most of the upper part was unsupported by the sand. According to Chevrier (fig. 13), a chamber would have been built, and the sand would have been taken through a hole in the bottom. The obelisk would then have been slid on the surface of the sand until it rested at an angle of 34 degrees. At that point, it would have been pulled up to a vertical position by means of ropes. [11] This modification of the theory proposed by Engelbach is plausible, the more so since Chevrier

PLATE 5. Possible reconstruction of the erection of one of Hatshepsut's obelisks as suggested by Engelbach, cf. fig. 13

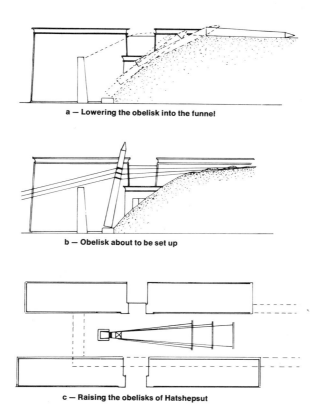

a — Lowering the obelisk into the funnel

b — Obelisk about to be set up

c — Raising the obelisks of Hatshepsut

FIGURE 13. Setting up an obelisk (Chevrier)

had been accustomed to dealing with the problems of setting up large stone monuments during his many years of work in the temples of Karnak.

The successful erection of monuments of such great weight and slender form is not so easy in practice as in theory. The obelisk of Tuthmosis I in Karnak, the smallest still standing in Egypt, can be observed to be leaning slightly, but no engineer at Karnak is as yet prepared to correct this fault. I remember that it took two whole seasons to dismantle and re-erect a column about 19.8 meters high, one of ten raised by the Ethiopian king Taharka (689–664 B.C.) in the first court of the Temple of Amun-Re at Karnak. When the job was completed, Chevrier stood on top of the column surrounded by flags, while the workmen on the ground applauded the achievement.[12]

In addition to the mechanics of the extraction and erection of obelisks, other questions relate to their decoration. The Unfinished Obelisk gives no indication of when or how this was done, but another, smaller unfinished obelisk in the region of Aswan helps provide answers. This is an obelisk of Sethos I (1318–1304 B.C.), which still lies in the quarry of Gebel Simaan on the west bank of the Nile, opposite Aswan (plate 6). Its pyramidion is partly decorated, albeit on only three sides. This demonstrates that in some cases the decoration was begun while the obelisk was still in the quarry. When the decoration would have been finished is uncertain, since the obelisk was abandoned.

The obelisk of Tuthmosis III now in the Piazza San Giovanni in Laterano and that of Sethos I in the Piazza del Popolo, both in Rome, were only partly decorated by the sovereigns responsible for their quarrying and, significantly, each on only three sides. The final decoration and the erection of the obelisks were left to their royal successors.

After an obelisk was extracted from the rock, it was fastened to a sled, and this sled remained in position until the obelisk had been erected on its pedestal. Thus only three sides were available for decoration at the quarry or in the royal atelier. It is unlikely that the decoration at all four sides would have been delayed until the obelisk was erected, but only then would the final, previously concealed side have been accessible.

The polish on the surface of the obelisks was achieved by pounding and grinding with diorite balls. The British Egyptologist W. M. Flinders Petrie (1853–1942) has suggested that tests to determine the evenness of the surface were made by pressing a flat plane smeared with red ocher against the surface to be smoothed. Any projecting point would be touched by the ocher and would then be smoothed down. During the time when the obelisks were being decorated, the Egyptians did not possess iron tools, and the available bronze tools were not adequate for the task. According to Petrie, emery was used for engraving inscriptions.

PLATE 6. Unfinished obelisk of Sethos I, lying in its quarry at Gebel Simaan near Aswan

"The difficult question is whether the cutting material [emery] was used as loose powder, or was set in the metal tool as separate teeth. . . . On the Egyptian examples there are long grooves in the faces of the cuts of both saws and drills; and grooves may be made by working a loose powder. But, further, the groove certainly seems to run spirally round a core, which would show that it was cut by a single point. . . . The large hieroglyphs on hard stones were cut by copper blades fed with emery, and sawn along the outlines by hand; the block between the cuts was broken out, and the floor of the sign was hammer-dressed, and finally ground down with emery." [13]

The ancient Egyptians used gold extensively in their monuments. The inner sarcophagus of Tutankhamun (1361–1352 b.c.) contained not less than 112 kilograms of gold. Doors, columns, and reliefs were sometimes completely covered with thin gold plates, and the pyramidions were usually covered with gold. [14]

On the base of her obelisk that still stands in Karnak, Hatshepsut recorded that "she made as her monument for her father
Amun, Lord of the Two Lands dwelling in Karnak, the making
for him of two great obelisks of solid red granite of the region of
the south; their upper halves gold of the best of all countries."
On Hatshepsut's obelisks and on those of her stepson Tuthmosis III, grooves with holes to affix plates of gold are clearly to
be seen on the pyramidions and on the upper parts of the
shafts. A stela in the tomb of a certain Djehuti who served as
treasurer to Hatshepsut describes her two obelisks "whose
height is 108 cubits [a cubit is roughly ½ meter] decorated completely with gold which fills the Two Lands with its rays."

The day of the erection of an obelisk must have been one of
excitement for the people of all the surrounding towns. It is
probable that the pharaoh himself would have been present on
such an occasion, as would the nobles and great personalities of
the realm, not to mention those who had taken part in the work
and were destined to be rewarded for its success (plate 7).
Amenhotep, the steward of Hatshepsut, received silver and
gold, the silver, which in ancient Egypt was more valued than
gold, amounting to 50 *deben* (about 4.5 kilograms). Humen, an
official who was charged with the erection of six obelisks for
Amenophis III, was favored in the "House of Rewarding" with
20 men, 50 arouras [18 acres] of land, and two weights of gold
and silver. Sometimes the pharaoh would lean out from the
"Window of Appearances" in the palace to supervise the decoration of his most worthy officials with collars of gold, to the
acclaim of their fellows.

No Egyptian records have survived which explain the
methods by which obelisks were quarried, moved, or erected.
Here and there among the papyri there are references to the
work needed to make an embankment or to fill a chamber with
sand or to erect a colossal monument. There is a text (in Papyrus
Anastasi I in the British Museum) posed in the form of a problem set by a schoolmaster for his pupil, which refers to an em-

bankment of the type that may have been needed to erect an obelisk. The embankment's dimensions are given as 730 cubits long and 55 cubits wide. It consists of 120 compartments filled with reeds and beams to a height of 60 cubits. The pupil is required to find the number of bricks necessary to build the compartments. (The answer is not supplied.) In another part of the same document, the teacher poses a problem concerning the erection of a colossal statue: "Empty the magazine that has been loaded with sand under the monument of thy Lord which has been brought from the Red Mountain. It makes 30 cubits stretched upon the ground, and 20 cubits in breadth, ———ed with 100 [?] chambers filled with sand from the river bank." The

PLATE 7. General, later Pharaoh, Haremhab being decorated with collars of gold for accomplishing some great feat

dimensions of the chambers are then given, and the pupil is asked how many men are needed to remove the sand in six hours. Again there is no answer. Although many passages in the two texts are obscure, they confirm that embankments were used in construction and that chambers filled with sand were also involved.[15]

The same papyrus also contains a question regarding the number of men needed to move an obelisk, but no dimensions are given. In another instance, when huge blocks were extracted from the Wadi Hammamat quarries, the number of people involved and their professions are known. An expedition sent there by Ramesses IV to bring back some large blocks consisted of the following:

Director of work (Ramessesnakht, High Priest of Amun)	1
Civil and military officers	9
Subordinate officers	362
Trained artificiers and artists	10
Quarrymen and stonecutters	130
Police	50
Slaves	2000
Infantry	5000
Men from Tura	900
Dead excluded from the total	800
	8462

This list shows that such enterprises required large numbers of people, both skilled and unskilled. Obviously the perils of the work were great, and many gave their lives for the success of these ventures.

Some references to the technical prowess of the ancient Egyptians occur in Greek and Roman literature. The Greek historian Herodotus in the fifth century B.C. described a monumental shrine designed to hold a statue, the external dimensions of which were 10.5 by 7.6 by 4.4 meters. He mentioned that the shrine "came from Elephantine, and took three years to bring to Sais, two thousand men, all of the pilot-class, having the task of conveying it." [16] Pliny the Elder, six centuries later, tells of a king, "Rhamsesis," who feared that the machinery being employed to raise an obelisk was not sufficiently strong and therefore ordered his own son to be tied to the summit of the obelisk in order to make his workmen take more care.[17] Engelbach, known for his sense of humor, said of Pliny's account that it "cannot fail to appeal to those who have had the fortune (?) to fall into the hands of an Egyptian dragoman. He must have livened up the visitors even in those days." Nevertheless, Engelbach remained sceptical about the king's threat. "If this 'Rhamsesis' was Ramesses II, the loss of a son would not have been vital, as he is known to have had over a hundred, to say nothing of several score daughters!" [18]

CHAPTER THREE

Heliopolis & Memphis–
The Old & Middle Kingdoms

FEW cities in the world have had so ancient a history and so glorious a past as Heliopolis and Memphis in Egypt (fig. 14). The latter was found by the first pharaoh (c. 3100 B.C.) as the center of national administration, and such it remained for more than eight centuries. Its god Ptah (fig. 15) was considered to be the creator of mankind and the patron of the arts, and he was regarded with great veneration from the earliest period until the rise of Christianity. The religious and political importance of Memphis led to its religious name *Hi-ku-Ptah*, "The Mansion of the *Ka* of Ptah," from which the Greek name of the whole country, *Aegyptos,* and in turn its English name, Egypt, were derived. After the Greeks under Alexander the Great (356–323 B.C.) conquered Egypt, Alexander's body was sent to Memphis but he was eventually buried in Alexandria, the Hellenistic city which he founded and which succeeded Memphis as the seat of government.

Heliopolis seems to have become important even earlier and it continued to be the most prominent center of Egyptian religion and science until near the end of the Ptolemaic period

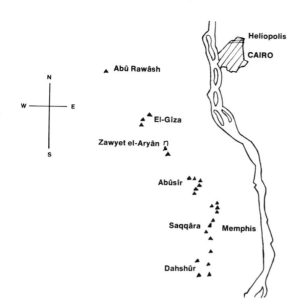

FIGURE 14
Memphis-Heliopolis and
the pyramid fields

(323–30 B.C.). Its learned priesthood attracted the attention of distinguished visitors from abroad. Herodotus drew much of his information from its priests. Earlier the Greek lawmaker Solon (640/635–c. 560 B.C.) and his fellow countryman, the scientist Pythagorus (sixth century B.C.), had visited Heliopolis and profited from the wisdom of that city. From their reports derived the Greek impression of Egypt reported by Plato (429–347 B.C.):

"We Greeks are in reality children compared with this people with traditions ten times older. And as nothing of precious remembrance of the past would long survive in our country, Egypt has recorded and kept eternally the wisdom of

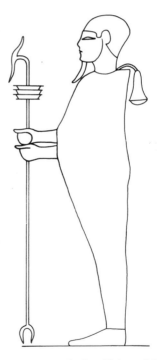

FIGURE 15. Ptah of Memphis

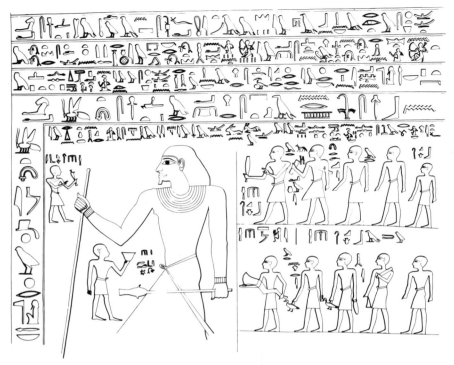

FIGURE 16. The inscription of Sabni

the old times. The walls of temples are covered with inscriptions and the priests have always under their own eyes that divine heritage. . . . The generations continue to transmit to successive generations these sacred things unchanged: songs, dances, rhythms, rituals, music, paintings, all coming from time immemorial when gods governed the earth in the dawn of civilization." [1]

Until relatively recently, no obelisk dated prior to the Middle Kingdom had been found in Heliopolis, and the obelisks of that period were often said to be the earliest true obelisks made. Egyptology is a field in which chance discovery may disprove an established theory; consequently Egyptologists rarely make unqualified statements but frequently salt their comments with "probably" and "perhaps." Some years ago, I was fortunate enough to discover an inscription which was to show that obelisks existed several centuries earlier.

The inscription (fig. 16) was made by Sabni, governor of the Aswan area under Pepi II (2269–2175 B.C.) of the Sixth Dynasty. In it, Sabni recorded that he went south to northern Nubia to construct two large ships for the transport of obelisks to Heliopolis. His inscription tells how he accomplished his mission successfully and brought back his workmen safely without loss of any kind, not even a single sandal! No trace of the obelisks to which Sabni referred has yet been found, but it is unlikely that he would have boasted of his achievements if the obelisks had not reached their destination safely. In all probability, they were quarried in the neighborhood of Aswan, and Sabni, as governor, may well have been in charge of their manufacture.[2]

In one of the inscriptions upon the walls of the burial chamber of the pyramid of Pepi I, father of the king under whom Sabni served, occurs the phrase *"Tekhenui en Re."* This phrase had previously been interpreted as "two pillars of Re," since neither contemporary inscriptions mentioning obelisks nor obelisks themselves were known to date to that time. With my discovery of Sabni's inscription, it is clear that the correct interpretation is "two *obelisks* of Re."

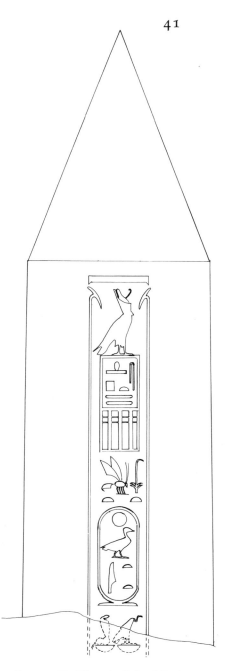

FIGURE 17. The obelisk of Teti

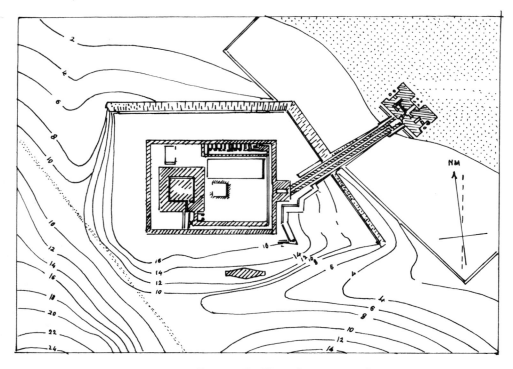

FIGURE 18. Plan of a sun temple

Owing to an accidental discovery in December 1972, it is now quite certain that obelisks were erected in Heliopolis even earlier. Muttawi Balbush, the chief inspector in the Egyptian Department of Antiquities, in making a few soundings around the surviving obelisk of Sesostris I, came upon two large blocks of quartzite, each carved with the name of Teti (2345–2333 B.C.), the father of Pepi I (fig. 17). One of the blocks was the lintel of a door; the other, the upper part of an obelisk which must once have been about 3 meters high. Only one side of the shaft is inscribed, and this preserves two of the king's names: "The Horus 'Sehetep-tawy,' the King of Upper and Lower Egypt; the Son of Re, Teti." Additional names of the king and probably some epithets are now lost. The lintel must have once belonged to a chapel built by Teti in Heliopolis, and the obelisk fragment must be part of one of a pair which would have been erected before Teti's chapel.[3]

At present, the obelisk of Teti is the earliest true royal obelisk, but chance may bring to light still more ancient remains. Prior to Teti's reign only obeliskoid constructions are known.

One of the most interesting stories to come down from the days of the ancient Egyptians is one related in the Westcar Papyrus, now in Berlin. It tells how a famous magician was asked to divert Cheops (2591–2566 B.C.), the builder of the Great Pyramid at Giza. To demonstrate his powers, the magician cut off the head of a goose, rejoined the head to the body, and then brought the goose back to life. When he was asked to foretell the future, the magician prophesied that the wife of the priest of the sun god would one day give birth to three children by the god, who would in their turns become kings of Egypt as the

FIGURE 19. Perspective of the sun temple, opposite, as seen from the north

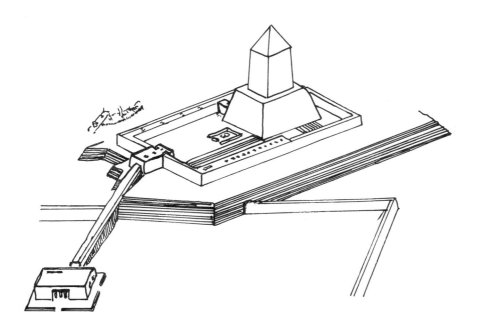

Fifth Dynasty.[4] The first part of the story, if true, credits great skill to the magicians of the time of Cheops, but that the prophecy took place is doubtful. Many such incidents appear in Egyptian literature but the prophecies were composed after the events had taken place, for propagandistic purposes and to provide explanations for historical events. In this case, the story reflects the special relationship between the pharaohs of the Fifth Dynasty and the sun god Re.

The Fifth Dynasty kings showed their devotion to the cult of the sun god by building sun temples[5] not far from their own mortuary temples on the plateau of Abu Sir, located to the north of Saqqara, the necropolis near Memphis. The sun temples have been almost completely destroyed, but systematic excavations by the German Egyptologists Ludwig Burchardt (1863–1938), have revealed the layout of one such complex: the sun temple of Neuserre (2449–2417 B.C.) (figs. 18, 19).

The temple itself was built on a platform on the edge of the plateau and was reached through an entrance porch on the cultivated area that would have been accessible by water only during the annual inundation. From the porch, the temple proper was reached by means of a causeway 100 meters long which ended in a second porch giving access to the temple compound, or temenos (80 by 110 meters). This consisted of an open court containing a large altar and places for sacrificial slaughter. Around the court were various corridors, storerooms, and chapels. Chapels contained beautiful reliefs. Some showed divinities personifying various districts, the Nile gods, and the seasons, along with animals and plants of an appropriate nature, all represented there to indicate the sun as the source of life. Other reliefs depicted the ceremonies of the king's Jubilee.

The dominant single feature of the entire temple was a large obeliskoid structure which stood upon a high truncated pyramid. This "obelisk" was not a monolith, like the later true obelisks, but was composed of separate blocks. It would have reached a height of 36 meters when complete, and its pyramidion would have stood some 56 meters above the court of the

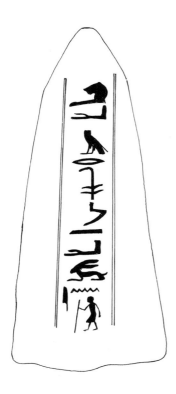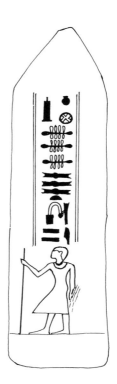

FIGURE 20. Obelisks of Uni (*left*) and Sheshi (*right*)

temple. The entire temple and the "obelisk" as well were
sheathed in white limestone, from which the rays of the sun
must have gleamed in splendor. The whole huge complex was
splendidly planned but of a type that was to be restricted to the
Fifth Dynasty only.

Beginning in the Fifth Dynasty a peculiar type of obelisk was
developed to mark the entrances to some tombs. These obelisks
were usually small and thin, made of limestone, and placed one
on each side of the tomb entrance. Examples of these are known
primarily from Memphis, Heliopolis, and Giza. Only the front
side of these obelisks was inscribed, usually with the name and
titles of the tomb owner. Those found in the Memphite cemeter-
ies belonged to important people, usually related to or serving
the royal family. One pair of obelisks was inscribed with the

name of "the scribe of the phylae of Heliopolis and of the troops, Sheshi" (fig. 20 right); another with that of "the vizier, Ptahhotep." Yet another pair bore the name of Neit, a queen of the Sixth Dynasty pharaoh Pepi II. Another pair of obelisks was inscribed with the name of "the governor and real overseer of the South, Uni (fig. 20 left)." Uni left a long inscription enumerating the great deeds which he accomplished under the first three kings of the Sixth Dynasty and telling how he was promoted from an obscure post to be governor of the South. Perhaps the most significant of these private obelisks was inscribed for "the unique friend and ritual priest, the one blessed by Anubis-on-his-mountain, Khenu, nicknamed Themi." [6] The mention of Anubis, a funerary god, suggests that this and similar obelisks were also considered to be funerary as well as solar in nature. During the Seventeenth Dynasty (1650–1570 B.C.) a pair of small obelisks bearing prayers addressed to the Gods of the Dead was set up before the tomb of King Nubkheperre Antef for the welfare of that king.

The Sixth Dynasty closed with the reign of a queen, and it was followed by a period of disintegration usually termed the First Intermediate Period. During most of this time, Egypt was divided into a number of relatively autonomous districts. After about a century and a half (or possibly only sixty years), this condition was ended by the actions of the nomarch, or district governor, of Thebes, who was able to reunite the whole country. With this event the Middle Kingdom began: an epoch of prosperity and great achievement which lasted for nearly three centuries.

Sesostris I, the second king of the Twelfth Dynasty, reigned for forty-five years and left his mark throughout Egypt. He seems to have built a new temple in Heliopolis in honor of the sun god. At the beginning of the present century, two fragments of this temple were found re-used in buildings in Cairo. The only part of the temple still standing is an obelisk raised as part of Sesostris I's building program.

Curiously, while the temple is almost completely destroyed,

records of the date of its construction and a plan of its parts still exist. In Berlin there is a much damaged roll of leather once used by a scribe for practice. On one side of this roll, the scribe copied a dedicatory inscription which Sesostris I may have had carved upon a stela at his temple in Heliopolis. The stela has never been found, and the temple itself has been destroyed; only the scribal exercise records the decision of the king to build a temple for the god Harakhti in the third year of his reign (1968 B.C.).[7] The second record is a plan of the temple carved upon a thin piece of stone of which some fragments remain. The plan shows the temple with the additions made by later kings. On it, the dimensions of the various parts of the temple are noted, and people charged with the work are mentioned. From the plan, it is possible to establish the original form and orientation of the temple at Heliopolis; the surviving obelisk once stood at the right of its entrance.[8]

The standing obelisk of Heliopolis is the oldest surviving obelisk (plate 8). It was one of a pair, its mate having fallen during the Middle Ages. Accounts of the pair are extant from various writers of the post-pharaonic period. The earliest may be a commentary on a chapter of Isaiah by Saint Epheaim (fourth century A.D.) in which he says that the cult of devils and the worship

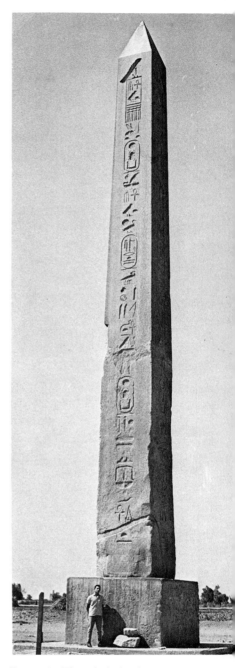

PLATE 8. The obelisk of Sesostris I at Heliopolis

of idols flourished in Heliopolis. In this place, he states:

"There are two great columns which excite admiration.

"Each of them is 60 cubits high and stands on a pedestal 10 cubits high. The cap which rests on the top of each of these columns is of white copper, and its weight is 1,000 pounds or even more. On these columns are depicted figures of the men and animals which were shown by their priestly character to contain the mysteries of paganism." [9]

The figures containing "the mysteries of paganism" were apparently on the copper caps. This is confirmed by an account given by the Arab historian Maqrizi (1364–1442), who said that the caps were like gold and that the figure of a man seated on a throne facing the rising sun was depicted on them. Another Arab historian, Yakut (early thirteenth century), also mentioned the obelisks, saying that people called them *Messalat Far'un*, "Pharaoh's Packing Needles."

The best information about these obelisks comes from Abd el-Latif, an Arab physician who traveled widely in the last quarter of the twelfth century. In the account of his journeys, he described the obelisks as square columns of pyramidal shape, 100 cubits high, standing on pedestals 10 cubits square and 10 cubits high. The top of each was covered with a copper cap in the shape of a funnel which hid the upper end of the shaft to a depth of 3 cubits. Owing to rain and the passage of time, the copper had oxidized, and the water running down from the cap had stained the shaft green. The whole surface of both obelisks was covered with inscriptions in the priestly character—that is, in hieroglyphs. He added that one of the obelisks was lying on the ground in two pieces.

While the dimensions of the obelisks are exaggerated, the general accuracy of Abd el-Latif's account of other events makes it likely that the second obelisk was already lying broken on the ground when he wrote. A later Arab historian, Muhammed Ibrahim Jaziri (A.D. 1263–1338), recorded that this obelisk fell on the fourth day of Ramadan (the month of fasting in the Moslem calendar) in the year 656 A.H. (A.D. 1258); he also said that 200 quintars of copper were removed from it, the copper being worth 10,000 dinars. However, the year in which the obelisk fell is generally believed to be 556 A.H. (A.D. 1158), which accords with Abd el-Latif's account. Most probably, the obelisk was intentionally overthrown by the local inhabitants, who thought that treasure might be found under it.[10]

The surviving obelisk is of red granite, 20.4 meters in height; the total weight is 121 tons. Recently a small change took place in its position. It was noticed that the base and a small part of the shaft were covered by water for some time each year. When the obelisk was first set up, it was much above the subterranean water level, but after almost forty centuries, the bed of the Nile and the level of the land had risen so that by 1950 the obelisk was in danger of collapse. The German firm of Krupp of Essen raised the obelisk and its base about 2 meters. The work was done under the supervision of Kamal el-Mallakh, then an architect with the Egyptian Department of Antiquities. The effort was a complete success, and the obelisk should remain above water for centuries to come.

Each side of the obelisk has a single column of inscriptions identical on all four faces. It reads: "Horus 'Living-in-Births,' King of Upper and Lower Egypt 'Kheperkare,' Two Ladies 'Living-in-Births,' Son of Re 'Sesostris,' beloved of the Souls of Heliopolis, living forever, Horus of Gold 'Living-in-Births,' the Good God 'Kheperkare.' The first occasion of the Jubilee, he made [it] to be given life forever." Included in this inscription are the five titles of Sesostris I, a pattern of names held by most kings after the Fifth Dynasty. Of these names, two are more important and are enclosed in cartouches or "royal rings." The first of these was his coronation name as "King of Upper and Lower Egypt," and the second his personal name as "the Son of Re."

The inscription also identifies the period when the obelisk was erected. The Jubilee of the king traditionally marked the thirtieth year of his reign, and since Sesostris I came to the throne in 1972 B.C., the obelisk was presumably erected for the festivities in the year 1942 B.C.

In March 1912, W. M. Flinders Petrie made some investigations in a field southeast of the obelisk of Sesostris I. There he found some two dozen fragments, some of which belonged to an obelisk that bore an inscription of Tuthmosis III augmented by inscriptions of Ramesses II. Examination of the fragments showed that this obelisk was the same size as that of Sesostris I, a fact which led Petrie to suggest that they might have formed a pair. Since Sesostris I had sufficient time to decorate a pair of obelisks in his own name, this suggestion seems unwarranted. Other fragments had parts of names which could have belonged to either Amenophis II or Tuthmosis IV, the son and grandson respectively of Tuthmosis III. The plan of the temple at Heliopolis was made during the reign of Amenophis II, and he is more likely to have raised obelisks there.[11]

The successors of Sesostris I were active rulers, but so far as is known, they did not erect any important structures in either Heliopolis or Memphis during the rest of the Middle Kingdom. The glory of that period faded, and it, like the Old Kingdom, was followed by a period of upheaval—the Second Intermediate Period (1786–1570 B.C.). During this time, a group or groups of Asiatics known as the Hyksos occupied part of Egypt, and the country was effectively divided again into small states. This situation continued for about a century.

CHAPTER FOUR

Thebes & Other Cities– The Eighteenth Dynasty

AMONG the classical writers who took a particular interest in Egypt and its obelisks was the Roman soldier and historian Ammianus Marcellinus (fourth century A.D.). He traveled in the country and greatly admired its monuments, and he was present while four obelisks were being transported from Egypt to Rome. After visiting Thebes, he wrote perceptively about its obelisks:

"In this city of Thebes, among many works of art and different structures recording the tales relating to the Egyptian deities, we saw several obelisks in their places, and others which had been thrown down and broken, which the ancient kings, when elated at some victory or at the general prosperity of their affairs had caused to be hewn out of the mountains in distant parts of the world, and erected in honor of the gods, to whom they solemnly consecrated them." [1]

The ruins of Thebes (fig. 21) now lie under, around, and opposite the modern town of Luxor, a city of about 60,000 inhabitants. Reaching Luxor either by train or plane, the visitor is struck by the vastness of its monuments. Upon close inspection, he is even more impressed by their splendor.

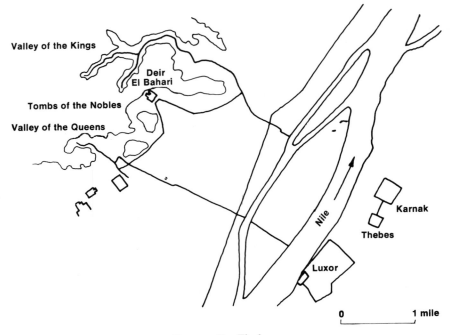

FIGURE 21. Thebes

On the east bank of the Nile was the City of the Living. In its midst (now north of Luxor) stood Karnak (fig. 22, plates 9, 10), a group of temples occupying an area of about 150 acres. Karnak was the national shrine of Egypt for more than twenty centuries, during which successive kings added temples and shrines, pylons and colonnades, statues and obelisks, a myriad of monuments in honor of the gods to whom they credited their victories. Throughout these temples two scenes recur: one showing the god Amun or Amun-Re (fig. 23) presenting the king with a sword with which he might smite his enemies, the other portraying the king offering the god rich tribute and prisoners captured during his victories.

In the southern suburb of the ancient city (now in the midst of the modern town) stood the Temple of Luxor with its lofty pylon and colonnades and its broad courts. This temple is the one most frequently visited in Egypt. Between Karnak and Luxor was an avenue of sphinxes along which were arranged the royal palaces and villas and the lesser buildings of the city of Thebes. The remains of these minor buildings lie completely hidden under the dwellings of successive generations who have occupied the site since.

On the west side of the Nile was the City of the Dead. For at least 2 miles along the edge of the desert there is a line of royal funerary temples; in the cliffs and valleys beyond, hundreds of tombs have been cut, some reaching deep into the rock. To the north lies the isolated and barren Valley of the Kings, where the sovereigns of Egypt and some of their nobles were buried, along with priceless treasure. To the south lies the Valley of the Queens, where the Mistresses of the Two Lands, together with several princes who died in their youth, had their resting places. In between are the hundreds of other tombs reserved for nobles who had served their royal masters. In these tombs,

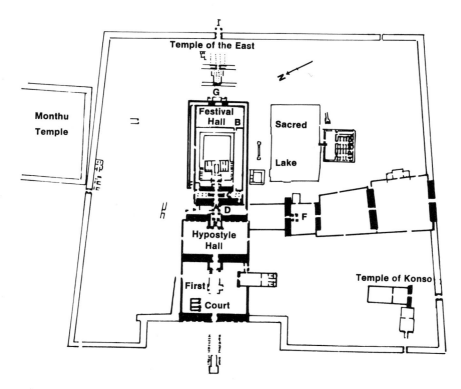

FIGURE 22. Plan of Karnak

PLATE 9
Aerial view of Karnak,
taken at the beginning
of the twentieth century

PLATE 10
A recent view of the Temple
of Karnak and its obelisks
reflected in the Sacred Lake

viziers, stewards, generals, sculptors, treasurers, priests, and countless others were eager to commemorate the roles they had played in their lifetimes. The tombs provide an endless source of information about the history of Egypt and the daily life of its citizens during its most important and prosperous period. Even the City of the Dead was not devoid of life, for it contained studios and workshops to provide tomb furnishings for the dead, as well as houses of artisans and palaces of kings, the former for convenience, the latter to keep an eye on the work that was intended to insure their immortality.

During the Old Kingdom and the First Intermediate Period, Thebes was simply the capital of the fourth nome (district) of Upper Egypt. At the end of the First Intermediate Period, the ruler of Thebes, as has been mentioned, re-established order throughout the land, ushering in the prosperous Middle King-

FIGURE 23. Amun-Re, king of the gods

dom. During the Second Intermediate Period, when the country was occupied by the invading Hyksos, it was again from Thebes that the savior of Egypt was to come. Ahmose (1570–1546 B.C.), who was responsible for the ultimate overthrow of the Hyksos, founded the Eighteenth Dynasty, the first of the three splendid dynasties which comprise the New Kingdom (1570–1085 B.C.).

During the reigns of Ahmose and his successors, the pharaohs considered themselves the masters of the world. They waged war far beyond the natural frontiers of Egypt and again and again were victorious. From these victories wealth poured into Egypt and the pharaohs embellished their capital with all manner of monuments, while their nobles made statues and stelae for themselves, each according to his means. As a result, Thebes became one of the most important centers of the civilized world. Even when the city had ceased to be the political capital, it continued as a significant religious center. The fame of the city even in its decline is preserved forever in the ninth book of the *Iliad:*

> Where in Egyptian Thebes the heaps of precious ingots gleam.
> . . . The hundred-gated Thebes, where twice ten score in martial state of valiant men with steeds and chariots march through each massy gate.[2]

The largest obelisks date to the Eighteenth Dynasty; some are still standing *in situ*, although many have been destroyed and others have been taken out of Egypt. Most of the obelisks once stood in the two great temples of Karnak and Luxor, but now only three remain.

Tuthmosis I, the third king of the Eighteenth Dynasty, was responsible for erecting the first pair of large obelisks at Thebes. During his reign and those of his daughter Hatshepsut and his grandson Tuthmosis III, Egypt was at the zenith of its power, and vast building projects and many successful campaigns were undertaken. Tuthmosis I was a great warrior; he fought against the Nubians in the south and the peoples of Asia. He was even able to bring the might of Egypt across the river Euphrates in Syria. In thanksgiving, he added greatly to the buildings in his capital.

The information about the building activities of Tuthmosis I is derived from inscriptions in the tomb of one of the king's officials, Aneni (tomb 81 in the Necropolis overlooking Thebes).[3] These tell how Tuthmosis I ascended the throne after Amenophis I and describe Aneni's own career. He reported that he built for his sovereign a great pylon with flagstaffs of cedar of Lebanon decorated with electrum (an amber-colored alloy of gold and silver) and a gateway having a door of Asian copper inlaid with gold. Aneni also provided an account of the transport and erection of the two obelisks of Tuthmosis I: "I saw to the erection of *two* [great] obelisks, . . . having built an august boat 120 cubits in length and 40 cubits in width in order to transport these obelisks; they arrived safe and sound, and landed at Karnak."

One of these obelisks still stands in the court between the Third and Fourth Pylons at Karnak, while parts of the other can be seen lying on the ground near its pedestal (plates 11, 12). The latter was still standing as late as the eighteenth century, when it was seen by the English traveler Richard Pococke.

Both obelisks are red granite. The standing one is 19.5 meters high, and its weight is estimated at 143 tons. Although it now leans a little, it is still stable. On each face the inscription begins with the names of the king in a single column. That of the west face tells that Tuthmosis I "made it as a monument for his father Amun-Re, foremost of the Two Lands, erecting for him two large obelisks at the double gate of the temple, the pyramidions

being of [electrum]. . . ." The inscriptions on the other faces continue in much the same fashion. About four centuries after the obelisk was erected, Ramesses IV (1166–1160 B.C.) added columns of inscriptions at either side of those of Tuthmosis I, but in turn Ramesses VI had his own name reset over that of Ramesses IV. The inscriptions of Ramesses IV/VI consist of stereotyped phrases recounting the glories of the king.

Tuthmosis I was followed on the throne by his son Tuthmosis II who, with his wife and half-sister Hatshepsut, reigned for about nine years. When Tuthmosis II died, he was followed by Tuthmosis III, his son by a minor wife. Hatshepsut first served as regent to the young king, but early in the reign of her stepson she proclaimed herself "king." Tuthmosis III served merely as co-regent during the long period when the queen ruled. Hatshepsut was represented wearing the traditional artificial beard, and she was sometimes referred to by a masculine pronoun. The scribes often seem to have been confused. For a queen to proclaim herself ruler, after the death of her husband and with a legitimate heir on the throne, was unprecedented. In order that the people, and especially the priesthood, should accept such a step, the queen tried to placate them by erecting great monuments and by publicizing her achievements. So too did her important officials. She built many temples in honor of local deities at various places both in Egypt and Nubia, and most particularly she honored Thebes.

In the Great Temple of Amun-Re at Karnak, Hatshepsut erected a huge sanctuary surrounded with many subsidiary chambers and set up two pairs of obelisks nearby. Unfortunately, most of these structures did not long survive her death and the accession to sole rule of Tuthmosis III. Sometime, probably late in his reign, the images and names of Hatshepsut were removed wherever they occurred, and many of her monuments were destroyed or concealed. In many cases, the name of Hat-

PLATE 11. The obelisk of Tuthmosis I, seen through the Hypostyle Hall of the Temple of Karnak

shepsut was replaced by that of Tuthmosis I, Tuthmosis II, or Tuthmosis III.

Only one of the four obelisks that Hatshepsut erected is still standing in its original place. A second one is broken, although most of the fragments exist. Of the other two only a few fragments are known. This latter pair was erected by the queen at the beginning of her reign in the eastern part of the temple of Karnak. When Tuthmosis III built his Festival Hall in this part of the temple, he had the obelisks incorporated into the temenos wall of his own structure and the names and images of the queen erased. Parts of the shafts and one of the pyramidions are still in Karnak; the other pyramidion is now in the Cairo Museum. On that one, the space which the image of the queen once occupied is now filled with two altars bearing flowers. The hands of the god which once embraced the figure of the queen now hold a scepter and the sign of life.

The other pair of obelisks was carved on the occasion of Hatshepsut's Jubilee, already mentioned, and they were set up to the east of those of her father in the area behind the Fourth Pylon beside the "noble gateway 'Amun, Great of Awe.' " The only obelisk of that queen yet standing can still be seen there, as well as the lower part of its mate, still resting upon its base. The top of this broken obelisk now lies near the Sacred Lake at Karnak, and the once inaccessible reliefs can now be inspected closely. Other fragments of this obelisk have traveled widely. Two came into the possession of the Museum of Fine Arts in Boston in 1875, and others are in Liverpool, Glasgow, and Sydney, Australia.

Like its broken companion, the standing obelisk of Hatshepsut is of red granite. It is 29.5 meters high and weighs 323 tons. This pair differs in many ways from other obelisks erected earlier and later. Apart from the usual decoration of the pyramidion, there are on the upper half of each face of each obelisk eight scenes on either side of the customary column of inscription (plate 13). Each scene contains a figure of the queen or her stepson Tuthmosis III in adoration of or making offerings to

PLATE 14. Amun-Re blessing Hatshepsut, showing the removal and restoration of the name and image of the god, from the pyramidion of her fallen obelisk at Karnak

Amun-Re (plates 14, 15). Not only the pyramidion but the scenes were adorned with electrum, so that almost the entire upper half of the obelisk gleamed in the sun. The damage suffered by these obelisks was not caused in an attempt to obliterate the name of the queen; rather they suffered from the attacks of the agents of Akhenaten (1379–1362 B.C.), who removed the name and image of Amun-Re. This defilement was reversed by the actions of Sethos I.

On the base of the standing obelisk is an inscription of thirty-two horizontal lines, eight to a side (plate 16). The text describes both the earthly and divine events which surrounded the erection of this pair of obelisks by Hatshepsut and the loyalty of that queen to her beloved god Amun-Re:

"She made as her monument for her father Amun . . . the making for him of two great obelisks of enduring granite from the south, their upper parts, being of electrum of the best of all lands, seen on the two sides of the river. Their rays flood the two lands when the sun-disk rises between them at its appearance on the horizon of heaven. I have done this with a loving heart for my father Amun after I entered unto his secret image

PLATE 15. Hatshepsut making an offering to and being embraced by Amun-Re

PLATE 16. Inscription on the base of the obelisk of Hatshepsut, recounting the events of its manufacture

on the First Occasion [of the Jubilee]. . . . There was not sleep for me because of his temple, and I did not turn aside from what he ordered. . . . I have not been neglected of the City of the Lord of the Universe, rather I have paid attention to it. I know that Karnak is the horizon [of heaven] upon earth, the august ascent of the First Occasion, the sacred eye of the Lord of the Universe.

"I was sitting in the palace and I remembered the One who created me; my heart directed me to make for him two obelisks of electrum, that their pyramidions might mingle with the sky amid the august pillared hall between the great pylons of [Tuthmosis I]. . . . They are [each] of one block of enduring granite without joint or flaw therein. My Majesty began work on them in Year 15, second month of Winter, day 1, continuing until Year 16, fourth month of Summer, day 30, making 7 months in cutting [them] from the mountain. I acted for him with a straightforward heart, as a king does for any god. It is my desire to make them for him, gilded with electrum. . . . I gave for them electrum of the first quality which I measured by the sack like grain. . . . Let not anyone who hears this say it is boasting which I have said, but rather say, 'How like her it is, she who is truthful to her father.' The god knows it in me [namely] Amun, Lord of the Thrones of the Two Lands. . . . I am his daughter in very truth, who glorifies him."

The other obelisk had a similar inscription of the same length, but parts of it are now lost. Enough can be read to know that it speaks of the blessings granted by Amun-Re to his beloved queen by granting her dominion over her neighbors and the produce of their lands:

"I am his excellent [heir] beloved of His Majesty [Amun-Re] who placed the kingship of Egypt, the deserts and all foreign lands under my sandals. My southern border is at the region of Punt . . . my eastern border at the marshes of Asia . . . my western border at the edge of the horizon. . . . I was brought myrrh of Punt, . . . all the august wonders of that country were brought to my palace in one lot . . . turquoise from the region of Sinai . . . and the tribute of Libya."

FIGURE 24
Graffito of Senenmut

Although the borders of Hatshepsut's kingdom are unknown, one of the greatest events of her reign was an expedition by sea to the distant land of Punt to obtain spice trees for her temple at Deir el-Bahari.

The officials who shared in the glory of Hatshepsut's reign spared no effort in singing her praises and lauding her achievements. For this reason, many of them shared the fate of their queen; most of their private monuments were either partly or wholly destroyed, with their own names as well as that of the queen erased.

Two of Hatshepsut's stewards were responsible for erecting her two pairs of obelisks. The steward who supervised the work on the first pair, those erected in the eastern part of the Temple of Karnak, was without doubt Senenmut, the single most important person of her reign. In addition, he planned the queen's mortuary temple at Deir el-Bahari. The titles he held reveal his intimate connection with the court and the queen: governor of the royal palace, superintendent of the private apartments, of the bathrooms and bedrooms. In one of his surviving inscriptions, Senenmut recorded: "I was the greatest of the great throughout the whole world. . . . What the South and the North contributed was under my seal . . . there was nothing since the beginning of time which I did not know." [4]

In Aswan, on the rocks opposite Elephantine, Senenmut had a most important inscription carved (fig. 24). There he is shown in adoration of Hatshepsut at a time before the queen had made herself "king." The inscription below their figures recorded Senenmut's coming to Aswan to begin work upon two obelisks for the feast of "Myriads of Years," possibly a coronation feast. These obelisks are the pair that is shown in the reliefs in Hatshepsut's mortuary temple at Deir el-Bahari, at a time when she had already become "king," and they must date from early in her reign.[5]

Although this pair of obelisks was subsequently destroyed, some idea of their decoration can be obtained from a relief at Deir el-Bahari, in which Hatshepsut is shown presenting them to Amun-Re. Each obelisk had a single column of hieroglyphs down each side, containing the usual stereotyped inscription.

The steward responsible for the second pair of Hatshepsut's obelisks, those she erected between the Fourth and Fifth Pylons of the Great Temple of Karnak on the occasion of her Jubilee, was called Amenhotep, and he probably succeeded Senenmut in that office. Amenhotep left three rock inscriptions in the Aswan area (fig. 25). In one he is styled "chief priest of Anukis [the goddess of the Island of Seheil]." In the second the title "chief of works in the House of Granite" is added. In the third Amenhotep is referred to as "the true king's acquaintance, his beloved, the controller of works on the two great obelisks, chief prophet of Khnum, Satis, and Anukis." In all three inscriptions most of the signs have been erased, but their outlines are still preserved and they can be read with little difficulty.

Tomb 73 in the Theban Necropolis is clearly dated to the reign of Hatshepsut. Since the decoration of the tomb was done on a layer of plaster, the owner's name, which has been erased throughout the tomb, cannot be read. In one scene the unidentified tomb owner is shown in front of two obelisks and other objects, followed by two rows of attendants. The accompanying inscription refers to him as "the noble who carried out the work on the two large obelisks in the Temple of Amun at Karnak." The tomb owner recounted that he was rewarded with silver and gold; "the silver amounted to 50 *deben* [4.5 kilograms]"—a liberal reward indeed. Judging from the scene, the tomb owner was charged with the work on two of Hatshepsut's obelisks, certainly from the Aswan area. Since important people working at Aswan were given titles, perhaps only honorary, in the priesthood of the local divinities, I surmised that the owner of Tomb 73 was none other than the Amenhotep of the three inscriptions at Aswan. That the obelisks represented in tomb 73

FIGURE 25. Graffito of Amenhotep

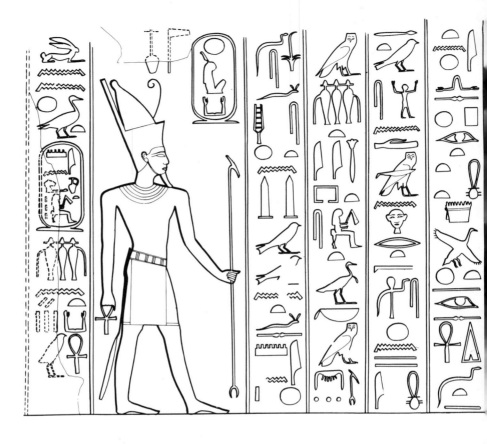

Figure 26. Block from the red quartzite shrine of Hatshepsut

were the second pair erected by Hatshepsut seems certain, since Senenmut was clearly in charge of the first pair.[6]

Some other references to the obelisks of Hatshepsut have survived. On one of the blocks of her red quartzite shrine at Karnak (fig. 26) is a scene of the queen offering two obelisks to Amun-Re: "The King himself [sic] erected two large obelisks for her father Amun-Re before the august columned hall, wrought very much with electrum. Their heights pierce the sky and make illumination for the Two Lands like the sun-disk; . . ." It is unknown which pair of obelisks is meant, but the mention of the "columned hall" suggests the second pair which were raised near the columned hall of Tuthmosis I.

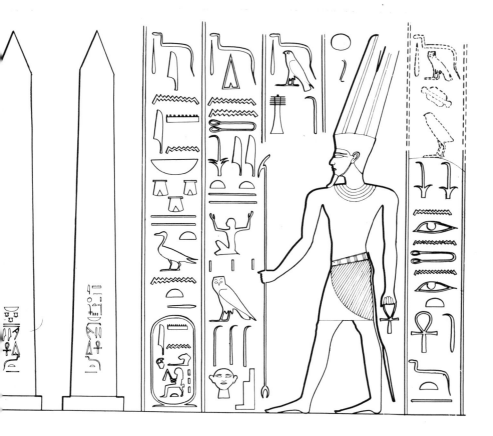

The so-called Northhampton Stela found in Tomb II of the Theban Necropolis belonged to Djehuti, treasurer during the reign of Hatshepsut.[7] On the stela are enumerated the various tasks with which Djehuti was charged, including work on a pair of obelisks: "I acted as a chief giving orders. I led the craftsmen to do work on two large obelisks, their height being 108 cubits [56.7 meters], covered in their totality with electrum. The Two Lands are filled with their rays. . . ." It is not known which pair is meant. The description does not fit the second pair, one of which is still standing. The height of the first pair is not known, which leaves the possibility that this could be the pair described, but Engelbach did not believe that this was the case, since an obelisk of such height could not have existed for technical reasons. It is quite possible that the figure is in error.

When Hatshepsut died, her co-regent and successor, Tuthmosis III, was already a grown man, and he soon showed his talents as warrior, administrator, and builder. Under him the government became highly centralized, and this provided the internal stability which enabled him to lead successful campaigns of foreign conquest. The plunder thus acquired gave him the means to erect more buildings than any previous king had done. Tuthmosis III set up at least seven obelisks in Karnak and two more in Heliopolis, but none of these still stands in its original place. They seem to have been erected for his first five Jubilees, celebrated successively in the thirtieth, thirty-fourth, thirty-seventh, fortieth, and forty-third years of his reign; although two of the obelisks (apparently, from the numbers written below, meant to represent two *pairs* of his obelisks at Karnak) are depicted in a scene showing the treasure which he offered to Amun-Re in celebration of the military campaigns in which the god had given him success.

The pair of obelisks carved for the celebration of the first Jubilee seems to have been made under the supervision of Puyemre, a high official who served both Hatshepsut and Tuthmosis III (fig. 27). In Puyemre's vast tomb (39 in the Theban Necropolis) is a scene of particular importance; it shows Puyemre seated facing two rows of officials and a pair of obelisks.[8] Above him is an inscription: "Inspection of the great and excellent monuments which the King of Upper and Lower Egypt, the Lord of the Two Lands Menkheperre [Tuthmosis III] made for his father Amun of Karnak in silver, gold, and every precious stone by the noble and governor, the beloved god's father, Puyemre." The officials are styled "overseers of craftsmen of the Temple of Amun, Lord of Karnak," and "overseers of works" in the same temple. The inscriptions on the obelisks do not differ from those usually placed on such monuments. The scene is described as the "introduction of officials and overseers of works, who say in the presence of this official, 'Every heart is delighted with all the work which you brought about in order to erect them' [the obelisks]."

Six of the obelisks erected by Tuthmosis III were made under the supervision of the first herald of the king, Yamunedjeh, who left a rock inscription on the Island of Seheil near Aswan, perhaps near where he quarried the obelisks. In his tomb (84 of the Theban Necropolis), this official boasted that he witnessed the erection of two pairs of obelisks in honor of Amun and a third pair in honor of Atum, lord of Heliopolis.[9] Since the pair in honor of Atum was erected in Heliopolis for the third occasion of the Jubilee, those dedicated to Amun may have been erected in Karnak for the celebration of the first and second or the second and fourth Jubilees.

One other official of Tuthmosis III, Mennkheperresonb, the high priest of Amun and controller of works in the sanctuaries of Amun, claims to have participated in the erection of the king's obelisks.[10] In one of his tombs (86 in the Theban Necropolis) is a scene in which he is "inspecting the work of the Temple of Amun and the activities of the craftsmen." In the scene, an inscription reads: "I was witness when His Majesty erected many obelisks and flagstaffs." Undoubtedly he did this in his dual capacity as supervisor of works in the temple and as chief priest.

Of the three pairs of obelisks erected at Karnak, one stood to the south of the Seventh Pylon; the upper part of one of these is now in Istanbul, while fragments of its mate remain at Karnak. A second pair stood to the west of the obelisks raised by Tuthmosis III's grandfather Tuthmosis I. The pedestals of these were recently unearthed from beneath the foundations of the Third Pylon. In building this pylon, Amenophis III (the great-grandson of Tuthmosis III) must have taken down the obelisks and reused them elsewhere. The placement of the third pair of obelisks is unknown, and no trace of them exists.

The seventh and last of the Karnak obelisks of Tuthmosis III, a single one, is the largest surviving obelisk, with a height of 36 meters. Only its foundation remains in the eastern part of the

FIGURE 27. Puyemre and the obelisks of Tuthmosis III

Great Temple at Karnak. The base is lost, and the shaft was removed to Rome in antiquity, where it now stands in the Piazza
San Giovanni in Laterano.

On this obelisk, Tuthmosis III referred to its erection as a soli-
tary obelisk, instead of the usual pair. The question remains as
to whether the king had once planned for this to be but a part of
a pair—a reasonable hypothesis.

The Unfinished Obelisk at Aswan, previously discussed, remains without date or history. Of it, Engelbach wrote: "As to
the date of the obelisk, there is very little indication of it; since
it was a failure, it was in nobody's interest to record it. It may
have been of the time of [Hatshepsut] (i.e., about 1500 B.C.),
since large obelisks seem to have been the rule in her time. Further, the outline of a smaller obelisk drawn upon the surface of
the large one . . . , which can be seen well just after sunrise, is
almost exactly the same dimensions as that now known as the
Lateran obelisk at Rome, the work of Tuthmosis III, her co-
regent and successor. These evidences of date should, however,
be accepted with a good deal of caution." [11]

This theory of Engelbach's seems to find support in an inscription carved near the entrance to the quarry of the Unfinished Obelisk, some 150 meters from the obelisk.[12] It was
carved by the overseer of the priests of Onuris, Min, known
through his tomb (109 in the Theban Necropolis) to have lived
during the reign of Tuthmosis III. Min's inscription is remote
from others in the area but close to the Unfinished Obelisk, a
fact which suggests that he might at some time have been concerned with it. Min does not seem to have been the one who
began work on the obelisk, however. Under certain lighting, his
inscription can be clearly seen to have been carved over a still
earlier one. It is impossible to decipher the earlier inscription,
but it is tempting to consider it to have been made during the
reign of Hatshepsut and later erased, as were the inscriptions of
many of her followers. If this conclusion is correct, Min would
have been the official in charge of removing from the Unfinished Obelisk a smaller one to be the companion of the single

obelisk of Tuthmosis III, and in that case it is possible that he was also charged with the completion of the latter.

After a long and glorious reign, such as Egypt had rarely known, Tuthmosis III died, to be succeeded by his son Amenophis II. Although he also was a great warrior and builder, his accomplishments have been overshadowed by the fame of his father. Amenophis II may have had obelisks erected in Heliopolis in front of the temple which he built there, but only fragments have been discovered. On the island of Elephantine many blocks bearing his names were found, and a pair of his obelisks made of granite was also unearthed there. One of these, about 2.2 meters high, was presented in 1838 by Mohammed Ali, viceroy of Egypt, to Algernon, fourth duke of Northumberland and is now in Alnwick Castle in Durham, England. The upper part of its mate was found being used as the threshold of a house in a village on the north side of Elephantine. It was removed in 1920 and is now in the Cairo Museum. Both obelisks are decorated on one side only. The one in Alnwick Castle shows the king making offerings and bears the inscription "[Amenophis II] made as his monument to his father Khnum-Re, the making for him of two obelisks of the Altar-of-Re. . . ."

Tuthmosis IV, son and successor of Amenophis II, also built at Elephantine. He too seems to have erected two obelisks, although only the lower part of one has been recovered. Found on the island, it was later added to the collection of the Cairo Museum. Like those of Amenophis II, it has an inscription on one face only: "He made as his monument to his father Khnum, the making for him of two obelisks of the Altar-of-Re. . . ." This pair, as well as that of Amenophis II, may well have stood in a solar chapel in which an altar was the main focus of worship.[13]

Amenophis III succeeded to the throne of his father Tuthmosis IV. During his reign, the country enjoyed its most peaceful days, thanks to his predecessors who had established the might of Egypt among its neighbors. Blessed with prosperity and an increasing sophistication, Amenophis III was able to construct elegant temples in many places in Egypt and the Sudan, but it was to Thebes that he gave his greatest attention, making it the most magnificent city of what was then the civilized world.

No obelisk of the reign of Amenophis III is still standing, but in front of the Temple of Monthu (or Monthu-Re), the god of war, on the north of Karnak, there are still to be seen two pedestals and fragments of the obelisks which Amenophis III raised upon them. Judging from the dimensions of these fragments, the obelisks must have been more than 19 meters high. The inscriptions on them are too damaged to be read; undoubtedly they spoke of the king and his piety towards Monthu.

It is unlikely that Amenophis III would have failed to erect obelisks in honor of Amun-Re, whom he especially favored. On the Third Pylon which he constructed at Karnak, there is a long inscription enumerating the buildings which Amenophis erected, including obelisks. Obelisks are also mentioned on huge stela which he set up in his funerary temple at Thebes. Where these obelisks were erected is unknown.

Just prior to 1950, I was fortunate enough to discover an inscription of fourteen lines on the rocks of a small island in the river to the east of the Aswan Museum on the island of Elephantine (plate 17).[14] It had been carved by Humen, the overseer of builders of Amun, and recorded his work:

"I controlled [the work on] six obelisks for His Majesty, and His Majesty gave me two weights [?] of gold and silver. I was favored in the House of Rewarding with 20 men and 50 arouras [18 acres] of land. . . . I was a vigilant controller who did not sleep and who was not slack concerning what was laid in his charge, whom the king appointed to an important office in order to control for him great works, the heart [of the king] being confident as [Humen] returned when he had achieved [his task], for, [although] this land was provided with experts and controllers, there was none who could equal him in respect of his ability, namely the overseer of builders of Amun, Humen."

Since Humen was controller of the works of the god Amun,

PLATE 17. The rock inscription of Humen recording the procurement of six obelisks

the six obelisks with which he was concerned were undoubtedly destined for the temples of Thebes, and in particular the Great Temple of Amun-Re at Karnak. While the account of his work is plausible, the statement that no one among all the experts of Egypt could equal him in ability is somewhat hard to believe.

No king's name appears in the inscription, but the name of

the god Amun occurs twice, and in both cases it has been erased. This erasure probably took place during the reign of Akhenaten; the inscription was undoubtedly carved at a date prior to that reign. Since the people involved in the work on the obelisks of earlier kings are known, it is possible to attribute to Humen the obelisks of the reign of Amenophis III. As that king's buildings surpassed much of what was done before him, it is quite conceivable that he would have ordered six obelisks to be made at the same time.

The son and successor of Amenophis III, Amenophis IV, after reigning a few years changed his name, which meant "Amun-is-satisfied," to Akhenaten, "Beneficial-to-Aten." The change

FIGURE 28
Neferhotep at the temple

reflects the attitude which this king adopted toward Thebes and its god. After spending the first years of his reign at Thebes, he abandoned the city and moved to Amarna in Middle Egypt to devote his time to the adoration of his new god, who was symbolized by the sun disk, or Aten. In the face of the protest of the priesthood of Amun-Re, Akhenaten ordered the proscription of their god and the erasure of his name and image wherever either might occur. Men were sent into every temple and tomb; even graffiti did not escape the king's wrath. The obliteration was not an easy task, for the name of Amun occurred in tens of thousands of instances. The obelisks of Thebes were numerous, but the agents of Akhenaten took the trouble to scale them all, and even there, their hammers removed the reviled god's name and images.

Although the religion of Akhenaten was solar in origin and form, and in it the *benben* stone, or pyramidion, played an important role, only one fragment of an obelisk is known from his reign; this was recently unearthed from the First Court of the Temple of Amun-Re at Karnak. Too little of the inscription survives to give an idea of its original text, but the obelisk was undoubtedly erected in honor of the Aten, the divine symbol to whom Akhenaten devoted his life.

Akhenaten's successors, Smenekhkare, Tutankhamen, and Ay, were relatively unimportant kings, and no obelisk bearing any of their names has been found. Dating from one of their reigns, probably that of Ay, is an interesting scene in tomb 49 of the Theban Necropolis which belonged to Neferhotep, chief scribe of Amun.[15] The scribe and his wife are shown at the great Temple of Amun-Re (fig. 28). It has been suggested that the building represented is the eastern façade of the Great Temple with the single obelisk of Thutmosis III,[16] but this seems unlikely. There are no pylons in that area of the temple, yet pylons are clearly visible in the picture. In fact, the artist has shown the Third Pylon—at that time the front of the temple—with only one of the many obelisks between it and the Fourth Pylon which was the front of the inner temple. Neferhotep himself was not admitted to this inner shrine, and he could only receive a bouquet from a priest who stood on the porch before it.

After the upheaval caused by the followers of Akhenaten, Egypt's empire was severely weakened, and his successors on the throne were not able enough to repair the situation. It was left to Haremhab (1348–1320 B.C.), the last king of the Eighteenth Dynasty, to restore the fortunes of Egypt. In Karnak, he erected several buildings, including the Ninth and Tenth Pylons, often using stone removed from the monuments of his predecessors, especially those of the hated Akhenaten. A number of small obelisks belonging to Haremhab have come to light. Two fragments of these were found in the so-called Cachette of Karnak, a pit where they were thrown along with hundreds of statues and fragments removed from the over-crowded halls of the temple. A third fragment was found re-used in the eastern part of the Great Temple, while a fourth fragment was acquired from an antiquities dealer.[17] Recently the Franco-Egyptian Center at Karnak unearthed still another fragment. The inscriptions are conventional and of little impor-tance.

CHAPTER FIVE

Piramesse & Other Cities—
The Ramesside Period & Later

THE Ramesside kings of the Nineteenth and Twentieth dynasties came from the eastern part of the Delta (fig. 29). The founder of the Nineteenth Dynasty, Ramesses I (1320–1318 B.C.), was an old man when he came to the throne, and he reigned for only one year and a few months. His son Sethos I, who succeeded him, reigned for more than ten years. During his reign he favored the town of Avaris, at a site near his birthplace, where he erected a chapel to his patron deity Seth, a god not very popular until that time. The king also built a palace nearby, where he spent some time each year.

In earlier centuries, Avaris had been of such importance that the Hyksos conquerors of Egypt chose it as their capital during the Second Intermediate Period. In the wars by which the Egyptians expelled the Hyksos, the town must have suffered greatly and only in the reign of Sethos I did it regain some of its importance. Its real prominence came with the reign of Sethos I's son and successor, Ramesses II, who chose it to be the capital of Egypt. He renamed it Piramesse-Meramun, "The Domain of Ramesses, beloved of Amun." In this capital, Ramesses II constructed sumptuous palaces adorned with all the skills of the Egyptians. Around these were built the villas of the members of the royal family and those of the great officials of the court. In the various parts of Piramesse were erected barracks and workshops, but even more numerous were the temples of the gods. Not only the great deities of Egypt but also the gods of the various districts of the country and even those of foreign countries had their shrines there. Ramesses II tried to make his new capital the rival of the great cities of Egypt, even of Thebes itself.

Descriptions of the city of Piramesse are preserved, telling of its beauty, size, and prosperity. One was given by a certain scribe Pebesa in a letter to his superior:

"[Piramesse] the residence pleasant to live in: its country-side is full of everything good, and it has food and victuals every day. Its ponds have fishes, its pools have birds. Its meadows are verdant with herbage. . . . pomegranates, apples, and olives; figs of the orchard, and mellow wine of Kankeme surpassing honey. . . . Its ships sail forth and moor, (so that) food and victuals are in it every day. Joy dwells within it, and no one says, 'Would that (I had) unto it. The small in it are like the great. Come let us celebrate for it its festivals of heaven and its calendar festivals. . . . Dwell, be happy and stride freely about without stirring thence, [Ramesses-Meramun], the God." [1]

It is strange that a town of such importance as Piramesse, capital of Egypt for over two centuries, cannot now be located with certainty. The city was long identified with the ruins of Tanis,[2] because of the latter's huge monuments; however, many of these were brought there from earlier cities. In the Delta, stone was scarce, and many monuments had more than one home. The quarries were distant, and it was easier to "quarry" ancient sites than to obtain new stone. While the ruins of Tanis (plate 18) contain monuments once erected at Piramesse, those ruins do not overlay the city of Ramesses. The site now accepted by most scholars as being the remains of Piramesse lies under and around the obscure village of Qantir, about 30 kilometers south of Tanis.[3]

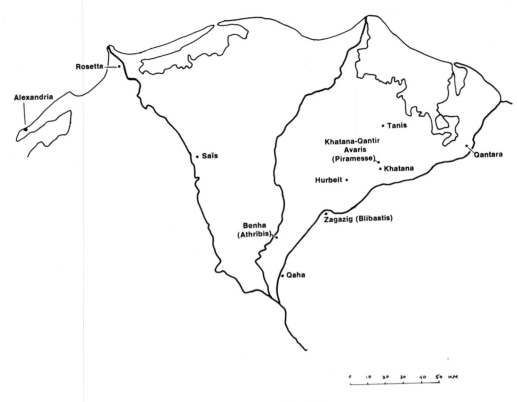

FIGURE 29. The Delta

Although only a few objects and blocks have been recovered from that site, the remains show unmistakable indications of the presence of palaces of Ramesses II and his successors. In addition, there are signs of the temples dedicated to the various gods of Piramesse. It seems certain that the Ramesside monuments of Qantir were dismantled and their blocks re-used to embellish later foundations, especially that of Tanis.

Among the approximately 800 rock inscriptions in the region of Aswan are some ten carved in the form of stelae, usually dealing with wars against the South. Two of these stelae, both dated to Year 9 of Sethos I and located near the Unfinished Obelisk, concern that king's building activities.[4] One stela mentions the production of huge statues; the second mentions both statues and obelisks. This second stela shows Sethos I burning incense before the gods of the Aswan area: Khnum, Satet, and Anukis. Below this scene are ten lines of text, the first seven of which give the date, the name of the king, and various laudatory epithets. The last three lines record the work done: "His Majesty (life, health, prosperity!) ordered to charge numerous workmen much work to make very great obelisks and great and wonderful statues in the name of His Majesty (life, health, prosperity!)." By Year 9 of his reign Sethos I had finished his wars against his neighbors and erected most of his buildings and so could turn his attention to the making of statues and obelisks for their embellishment.

Across the Nile from Aswan is a vast quartzite quarry lying between the ancient cemetery at Qubbet el-Hawa and the Monastery of St. Simeon. Quarrying is evident at various places, and numerous embankments extend toward the river. At the upper end of one of these embankments, some 10 meters in width, is the top part of an obelisk with its pyramidion.[5] Three sides of the shaft are partly decorated, while the fourth is barely even polished. On each of the decorated sides, Sethos I is shown

PLATE 18. The ruins of Tanis, with fallen obelisks of Ramesses II

kneeling and making offerings to one of the solar gods: the falcon-headed Harakhti, the Rising Sun; Atum with his double crown, the Setting Sun; and possibly Shu, the son of Re. Most probably the obelisk was planned for erection in Heliopolis.

Sethos I paid great attention to Heliopolis. Although none of his monuments survives, there are many indications of his building activities there. Most important is a model of a gateway which was added to the temple of Heliopolis (plates 19, 20). The model was reportedly found in 1875 in the ruins at Tell el-Yahudiya, some 20 miles northwest of Heliopolis, and it was later acquired by Major Henry H. Gorringe (1841–1885), to whom was entrusted the removal and re-erection of the New York obelisk. The model now belongs to the Brooklyn (N.Y.) Museum.

Only the base of the model is preserved; it is 28 centimeters high, 112 centimeters wide, and 87.5 centimeters deep. On the top are carved steps and a number of indentations to hold mod-

PLATE 19. Model made by Sethos I of a façade of a temple at Heliopolis, before restoration

PLATE 20. Model of Sethos I, after reconstruction of the missing parts

els of the various parts of the temple. On the sides are a series of reliefs showing Sethos I making offerings to the solar gods: Re-Harakhti, Kheperi, and Atum. The inscription on the right side gives an impression of what the model and the building it represented once were like. "The Good God [Sethos I] who makes monuments for his father Re-Harakhti, who has made a temple of good quartzite, [with] two pylon towers of white, crystalline limestone, doors of bronze, a pair of flagstaffs of *mesdet*-stone, [and] a pair of obelisks of *bekhen*-stone, [basalt], established in Heliopolis, the horizon of heaven, at whose sight the souls of Heliopolis rejoice." [6]

Bernard Bothmer, the curator of the Department of Egyptian and Classical Art at the Brooklyn Museum, initiated the reconstruction of the model, and the work was undertaken by Alexander Badawy, an Egyptologist who has long studied the architecture of ancient Egypt. Guided by the indentations on the top of the model, the description on its side, and his detailed knowledge of Egyptian architecture, Badawy reconstructed a pylon with flagstaffs, and pairs of sphinxes, statues, and obelisks.

This large model may have been the only one of its kind, made to serve as an architect's model for some important building project, but so little remains at Heliopolis that the traces of the building it represented are now lost. The fate of Sethos I's building may be known, for a number of his monuments were removed to Alexandria during the Roman period. A sandstone doorjamb of Sethos I is still in that city's museum, and a large block bearing his name supports the monument called "Pompey's Pillar." This block was once set up in Heliopolis, perhaps to serve as the base of an obelisk, and was later brought to Alexandria for re-use.

It is probable that for several years before his death Sethos I associated his son Ramesses II with himself as co-regent. It is certain that Ramesses II ruled Egypt for sixty-seven years, a reign so long that one of his successors even wished to equal it. During his reign, Ramesses II conducted some military campaigns, but he was more famous for his building achievements than for his military operations. There is hardly any site of religious or military importance in Egypt at which Ramesses II did not erect some structure. He erected more obelisks than any other king, although most of them were not as large as those of his predecessors of the Eighteenth Dynasty. Of his obelisks, one is in a park in Cairo; several are in the Cairo Museum. Others lie near where they fell, and still others have been removed from Egypt altogether. Only one, that before the Luxor Temple, still stands in its original place.

At Heliopolis, Ramesses II must have erected at least two pairs of obelisks, but these were removed by the Caesars to adorn the city of Rome. Three of them are still in Rome, while a fourth is now in Florence.

In 1927, the German Egyptologist Siegfried Schott (1897–1971) noted a quartzite pedestal of an obelisk of Ramesses II in the ruins of Athribis, a Delta city of special religious importance.[7] After long study, Schott was able to locate its companion pedestal and a fragment of gray granite which formed part of an obelisk that had rested upon one of the pedestals. The second pedestal and the fragment of obelisk had been removed from the ruins of Athribis for re-use in the buildings of Fustat, the capital built by the Arabs when they conquered Egypt in the seventh century A.D. In his search for fragments, Schott located one among the collections of the Staatliche Museum of Berlin. Little can be deduced from the fragmentary inscriptions on the recovered shafts of the obelisk. The pedestals, now reunited in the Cairo Museum, show Ramesses II making offerings to local divinities and to two solar gods, Harakhti and Atum.

Twenty-three obelisks or fragments of obelisks were unearthed in the ruins of the Delta city of Tanis, all but one being inscribed with the name of Ramesses II.[8] This does not mean that Ramesses was responsible for making them; some still bear traces of earlier inscriptions. The French Egyptologist Pierre Montet (1885–1966), who excavated at Tanis for more than twenty-five years, made exhaustive studies of the obelisks. Ac-

cording to him, there were five pairs of obelisks at the Great
Temple of Tanis. One pair stood before the First Pylon, another
before the Second Pylon. The third and fourth pairs were set up
at the entrance to the Third Pylon. The fifth pair was re-used as
foundation blocks in the rear of the temple. The other obelisks
have no relation to one another. Since many of these obelisks
overlay monuments of kings later than Ramesses II, and some
indeed were re-used in foundations, it is obvious that such
obelisks were not originally intended for Tanis but may once
have adorned either Ramesses II's own capital at Piramesse or
some other city.

   Not much information can be gained from the inscriptions on
these obelisks; they tell of the valor of the king and of his victories over his enemies without reference to any particular
event. There is no mention of the occasions on which the obelisks were erected, although they may have been originally set
up for some of the fourteen Jubilees which Ramesses II celebrated.

   In 1958, it was noticed that Cairo, unlike many other great cities, did not have a single monument of the pharaonic period in
a square or park. It was then decided that a colossal statue of
Ramesses II at Memphis and an obelisk of his at Tanis should
be removed to Cairo. The colossus was placed in the square by
the railway station, where it is seen by tens of thousands of Egyptians each day (plate 21). The obelisk was placed in a small garden on the island of Zamalek, on the bank of the Nile opposite
the great hotels of the city. Later the obelisk was surrounded by
other monuments brought from Tanis. Although it is more than
13.5 meters high and rests on a rather high modern pedestal,
the obelisk looks small among its surrounding palm trees, the
minaret of a nearby mosque, and the Cairo Tower. Those who
placed the obelisk there seem to have desired to overshadow the

PLATE 21. The obelisk of Ramesses II as it stands on the Island of Zamalek,
   Cairo

ancient monument, even though the obelisks in other countries are often magnified by their surroundings. The position of the obelisk in Cairo recalls the biblical statement: "A prophet is not without honor save in his own country" (Matthew 13:57).

On each face of the Cairo obelisk is a column of inscriptions describing Ramesses II: (west) "The King, the son of Ptah who is pleased with victory, who makes great mounds of corpses of [Bedouin]"; (south) "The one who seizes all lands with valor and victory, who establishes the Land [of Egypt] again as it was at the First Occasion"; (east) "A Monthu among kings, who attacks hundreds of thousands, the strong one like Seth when he enters the fray"; (north) "The king who smites every land and plunders this land of Nubia." Such is the tenor of all the inscriptions on obelisks originally erected by Ramesses II at Piramesse.[9]

The old capital of Thebes was the place where Ramesses II erected his largest obelisks. He added to the Temple of Luxor a large court with a huge pylon. In front of the pylon at the entrance of its gateway, he placed six colossal statues of himself and a pair of obelisks (plate 22). Within the court which he built is a scene showing a procession approaching the façade of a temple. In fact, it is a picture of the very pylon which Ramesses had built, complete with its six statues, two obelisks, and masts (plate 23). The procession included thirteen of the king's sons, high officials, and fatted bulls, as well as the king's favorite wife, Nefertari, and several of his daughters. It is not surprising that some of his progeny are present, for among his children, Ramesses II numbered more than one hundred and fifty sons and daughters.

Of the two obelisks which Ramesses II placed before the pylon of the Luxor Temple, only one now remains in place (plate 24); the other was taken to Paris, where it forms the focus of the Place de la Concorde. The Luxor obelisk is made of red granite; it is 25 meters high and weighs some 254 tons. It stands on a huge pedestal with four large statues of baboons on the front and the back of the shaft, each baboon with its front legs raised in adoration of the sun. Each side of the shaft has at the top a representation of the king making offerings to Amun-Re, and, below, three columns of inscription, over half of each consisting of the king's titles. The text on the front or northern face of the obelisk is typical in having no reference to any particular event. The center column gives the usual dedicatory inscription. That to the right calls Ramesses "splendid of statues, great of monuments in the Southern Opet [Luxor], . . . making monuments in Thebes for the One." The column at left calls Ramesses "the sovereign, great of Jubilees like Tatenen, making monuments in Karnak for his father Amun-Re who placed him upon his throne. . . ."

Nothing is known about the official who was responsible for erecting the pair of obelisks at the Luxor Temple. Curiously, there is much detailed information concerning the career of the official who was in charge of setting up another, now fragmentary pair of obelisks of Ramesses II which once stood at Karnak: Bakenkhonsu, the high priest of Amun-Re, who served as director of works at Karnak. From the monuments which he left a résumé of his life can be reconstructed, and it is clear that he rose from relative obscurity to the foremost offices of the land:

"I will inform you of my character while I was on earth, in every office I administered since my birth: I passed four years as an infant; I passed twelve years as a youth, being chief of the training stable of Men . . . [Sethos I]; I acted as priest of Amun for four years; I acted as god's father for twelve years; I acted as third prophet of Amun for fifteen years. [Ramesses II] favored me and distinguished me because of my rare talents, appointing me High Priest of Amun for twenty-seven years." [10]

Bakenkhonsu recorded his achievements in the Great Temple of Karnak: "I made for [the king] the Temple of Ramesses-Meramun 'Who-Hears-Petitions' at the upper gate of the Domain of Amun. I set up granite obelisks therein, the tops of which reach the sky. . . ." The temple constructed by Bakenkhonsu is located next to the site of the single obelisk of Tuthmosis III in the eastern part of the Great Temple of Amun.

PLATE 22
The Temple of Luxor with its remaining obelisk,
colossi, and avenue of sphinxes

PLATE 23, opposite
Façade of the Temple of Luxor, as shown in a
scene in the court of the temple made by
Ramesses II

PLATE 24
Obelisk of Ramesses II at Luxor, showing the
dedicatory inscription and the baboons with
their front legs raised in adoration

There, as with many other kings, Ramesses was identified with Amun, and the image of the god-king was accessible to the common people bearing petitions. No obelisk of Ramesses II now stands in all of Karnak, but outside the temenos wall at the Eastern Gateway were found two pedestals, along with some fragments of obelisks. One of these bears the name of Ramesses II and they may have been part of the constructions of Baken-khonsu.[11]

On the Nile at the southern frontier of Egypt is Abu Simbel, the site of two temples carved out of the cliffs during the reign of Ramesses II and in recent years the subject of much interest and great activity, since the temples were raised some 62 meters to save them from the waters rising behind the Aswan High Dam. To the north of the great temple of Abu Simbel, just off its terrace, Ramesses II had carved into the rock a small chapel, unique in type. Its eastern façade takes the form of a false pylon with two towers, but without an entrance in the middle. Access to the unroofed chapel is gained through a door opening from the terrace. On its walls were carved scenes connected with the cult of the sun god. Within were a naos (enclosed chamber) and an altar; the former contained two statues, one a scarab, the other a baboon. Four more baboons stood in positions of adoration upon the high altar. At the northern corners of the altar stood a pair of obelisks. The eastern one of the pair associated Ramesses II with Harakhti, the Rising Sun; the western one styled the king "beloved of Atum"—the Setting Sun (plate 25).

From the reigns of the later Ramesside kings only three obelisks are known. One was raised by Merneptah, the son and successor of Ramesses II. It was fashioned of red granite, and two fragments of it are preserved. They were found in the town of Qaha in the southern Delta where they seem to have been brought during the Middle Ages. The town has no other remains of pharaonic date. The obelisk once had two columns of inscription on each face, giving the names of Merneptah and various standard formulas. One epithet is more important as

PLATE 25
The obelisks, naos, and statues
from the sun chapel at Abu
Simbel (now in the Cairo
Museum)

suggesting the probable original provenance of the obelisk: "Establishing Heliopolis anew for his creator."

Sethos II, the son of Merneptah and grandson of Ramesses II, erected a pair of small quartzite obelisks. One of these is still standing on its pedestal on the quay before the First Pylon of the Great Temple of Amun at Karnak; the other is lost. The decoration of the surviving obelisk consists merely of the name of

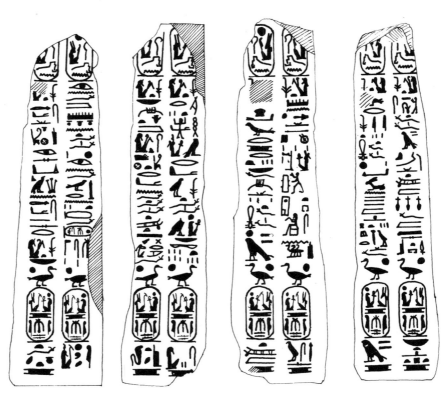

FIGURE 30. The obelisk of Ramesses IV

Sethos II repeated over and over. Compared with the obelisks of his predecessors, it is small and unimpressive.

Ramesses IV, the third king of the Twentieth Dynasty, was responsible for the last existing obelisk raised during the Ramesside period (fig. 30). It too is of quartzite, and only the lower part, some 1.56 meters, remains. The fragment was found re-used in a building in Cairo, and it was added to the collection of the Cairo Museum in 1887. Each side of the obelisk has two columns of inscriptions singing the praises of the king and styling him as beloved of the deities of Heliopolis. One of the sides, perhaps the intended front, gives the name of the obelisk. "[Ramesses IV] made as a monument to his father Re, the making for him of a large obelisk, the name of which is 'Ramesses, he-who-fashions-the-gods.' "[12] Names were often given to huge statues and obelisks, but this obelisk would not have been more than 2.5 meters high when complete. Despite the king's statement, it was not a "large obelisk." It is possible that it was actually part of a model like that of Sethos I.

Following the reigns of the Ramesside kings, Egypt was for the most part divided into smaller kingdoms, often ruled by foreign dynasties. During the Twenty-first Dynasty (1085–945 B.C.), the legitimate royal family resided at Tanis in the northeastern Delta; the high priest of Amun had effective control over Upper Egypt. The kings of the Twenty-second and Twenty-third dynasties were descendants of Libyan mercenaries. They may have resided at Tanis and were certainly buried there. Although some of the reigns were significant, Egypt was in a state of decline. The Twenty-fourth Dynasty centered at Athribis and lasted only five years; it was ended by the invasion of the Kushite kings from the Sudan who were to form the Twenty-fifth Dynasty. Although they had their capital far to the south, these Kings maintained a representative at Memphis. In fact, these conquerors may have been partly descended from Egyptian settlers in Nubia, and they erected temples to the Egyptian gods whom they considered to be their own.

The power of the kings of Kush was finally broken by the Assyrian empire when its armies invaded Egypt after 680 B.C. As an aftermath, a dynasty from the city of Sais in the western Delta was able to reunite the country and re-establish Egypt's independence and some of its glory. Known as "Saite" by virtue of their origins, the kings of the Twenty-sixth Dynasty attempted to revive old traditions of art and literature. They built extensively in their native town, which they made capital of all Egypt, but they also erected monuments in other parts of Egypt, especially the religious centers of Heliopolis and Thebes.

Psammetikos II, the third king of the dynasty, erected a pair of obelisks at Heliopolis, only one of which is preserved. It was taken by the Roman emperor Augustus from Heliopolis to Rome, where it remains. A second pair of obelisks was raised by Apries, who succeeded Psammetikos II. These obelisks once stood in the main temple of Sais. The goddess Neit was the chief deity of that city, but with her were also worshiped the solar gods, and thus Sais was "entitled" to have obelisks. At an unknown date, these obelisks were removed to Italy. Several fragments of one were used as part of an obelisk at Urbino, while the second stands in Rome.

The next king, Amasis, built a temple at Abydos, and a pair of obelisks at its entrance was probably set up by him. Part of one of these was unearthed in Minshah in Upper Egypt, to the north of Abydos.[13] At Abydos, Osiris, the God of the Dead, was the leading deity, but many of the solar gods were worshiped there as well. The obelisk of Amasis confirms this, for the king is mentioned as beloved of Osiris, Ptah-Sokar-Osiris, and the solar god Harakhti. The recovered fragment of this obelisk is a piece of granite 1.15 meters high, and the original monument must have stood not less than 2.5 meters high.

Following the Saite dynasty, the Persians invaded Egypt and formed the Twenty-seventh Dynasty (525–404 B.C.). In turn, they were replaced by the Twenty-eighth Dynasty, which consisted of a single king from Sais who ruled only six years and was followed by the Twenty-ninth Dynasty, which ruled from the Delta city of Mendes for eighteen years.

The kings of the Thirtieth Dynasty achieved a brief revival of Egyptian strength, and the last of them, Nectanebo II, raised three obelisks. The midsection of one of these is reported to have come from the neighborhood of Zagazig, a city in the eastern Delta. The fragment is of red granite, some 1.96 meters high, and it bears a column of inscriptions on each side. There the king is described as beloved of the "falcon pleased with life" and of Osiris in three of his manifestations: "the great bull, lord of Horbeit"; "the Mnevis in Horbeit"; and the second "the living soul of his sacred bark." [14] Horbeit was the capital of the eleventh nome of Lower Egypt. There an aspect of Horus (the falcon) was worshiped, and a sacred bull called the Mnevis was held in high esteem. A vast cemetery containing the huge sarcophagi for the mummies of these bulls was unearthed in 1954 at Abu Yassin, between Horbeit and Zagazig. Judging from its inscriptions, this small obelisk must once have stood either at Horbeit itself or perhaps at the cemetery of Abu Yassin.

The other obelisks of Nectanebo once formed a pair, three fragments of which are known. Two of these were seen by travelers during the eighteenth century and were removed at the end of that century by the savants who accompanied Napoleon Bonaparte during his unsuccessful campaign to conquer Egypt. These fragments were turned over to the British, along with the famous Rosetta Stone, in accordance with the Treaty of Capitulation which ended French presence in Egypt. The third fragment was later procured by the Cairo Museum, perhaps from a building in Cairo where it had been re-used. This fragment proved to fit with one of the fragments in the British Museum.

These obelisks of Nectanebo are made of schist and when complete would have been about 5.5 meters in height. On opposite faces of each of the obelisks are dedicatory inscriptions: "[Nectanebo II] made as his monument to his father Thoth, Lord of Ashmunein, the erecting for him of a large obelisk. . . ." On the remaining sides are additional references to Thoth, titulary deity of Ashmunein and its suburbs.[15] This city was the capital of the fifteenth nome of Upper Egypt and one of the main religious centers. Thoth, its chief god, was the patron of scribes and a god of writing; he was identified with Hermes by the Greeks. Not much is known of Ashmunein prior to the New Kingdom, but thereafter it flourished. Little can now be seen there, but much remains under the surface. The German Egyptologist Guenther Roeder (1881–1966) spent a decade excavating its ruins and was able to reconstruct the façade of a temple as it might have existed in the reign of Nectanebo II (fig. 31).[16]

Nectanebo II was the last native Egyptian king, although subsequent rulers retained the ancient titles. For nine years the Egyptians suffered under the cruel rule of the Persians, and when Alexander the Great invaded the country in 332 B.C. they looked upon him as a savior. After his death the country was

ruled by a long series of Greek kings, the males of the line bearing the name Ptolemy. Under the Ptolemies, Egypt enjoyed a
fair state of prosperity, and its new capital Alexandria became
famed as a center of Greek culture throughout the classical
world. The Ptolemies tried to placate the native populace by
erecting temples in many important religious centers. The temples of Dendera, Edfu and Philae are the results of this policy,
as are several small obelisks.

At the turn of the present century, the accidental discovery of

FIGURE 31. Reconstruction of a temple

a large number of Aramaic papyri dealing with a Jewish colony on the island of Elephantine during the fifth century B.C. prompted a French expedition to excavate on that island. Its members did not recover many papyri, but they did locate a cemetery of rams, animals sacred to the local god Khnum. Adjacent to one of the tombs in this cemetery there was discovered a chapel with an offering table and four obelisks.[17] No inscriptions were found in the chapel, on the offering table, or on the obelisks, but the last seem to have been covered with a layer of plaster which was painted or inscribed. Unfortunately, the plaster has fallen off, and the text is lost.

The builder of this chapel is not known. From the shape of the obelisks and the offering table, and given the proximity of the cemetery of rams which dates to the Ptolemaic period, it is probable that the chapel and its equipment belong to the same epoch. No trace of the chapel remains on the island. The offering table and two of the obelisks are in the Cairo Museum. A third obelisk is in the Metropolitan Museum of Art in New York. The fourth one seems to have been left on the island in fragments. The chapel may have been similar to those erected by Amenophis II and Tuthmosis IV on the island of Elephantine in which "obelisks of the altar of Re" were the principal objects of worship.

About five miles south of Elephantine lies the island of Philae, once known as the "Pearl of Egypt." When, toward the end of the nineteenth century, a dam was proposed that would cause the island to be submerged for part of each year, it was described as the "very damnable dam," by scholars who feared that Philae would vanish forever. In 1902, the first Aswan Dam was completed, and its height was increased in 1912 and again in 1934. Although the waters had covered more and more of the temples, they remained much as they were at the beginning of the century, save only that the colors have disappeared. However, Philae is now between the new High Dam and the old dam and is half submerged all year long. For this reason, the authorities have decided to dismantle the temples of Philae and re-erect them upon higher ground on a neighboring island called Agelkai. If suitable plans can be realized, the "Pearl of Egypt" will be restored and preserved forever more.

The temples on the island of Philae date mostly from the Greco-Roman period. The principal one was erected by Ptolemy II (285–246 B.C.) and decorated by him and his successors. In 1815, the English scholar W. J. Bankes, who had traveled extensively in the Near East, made soundings in front of the main temple at Philae. Among other important objects, he found a complete granite obelisk some 6.7 meters high and weighing about 6 tons. It was inscribed with the names of Ptolemy IX (116–81 B.C.), his sister Cleopatra, and his wife, also named Cleopatra. In 1819, Bankes employed the Italian strong man turned excavator, Giovanni Belzoni, to remove the obelisk from the island, and in due course it was placed on Bankes's estate in England. The lower half of a matching obelisk was also found; for a time it was left *in situ* but afterward was also taken to Bankes's estate. [18]

The hieroglyphic inscriptions on the obelisk are as conventional as those of many earlier ones. They mention Isis, the principal goddess of Philae, and her consort Osiris, as well as some of the solar gods. The king is described as "Horus the youth, rejoicing upon the throne of his father, holy image of the King of the Gods, chosen of Atum himself, lord of the Two Lands, the heir of the two gods, chosen of Ptah, who makes the rites of Amun-Re, King of the Gods, lord of the Thrones-of-the-Two-Lands, pre-eminent of Karnak, making to flourish those who dwell in the domain of Horus, beautiful image in the sanctuaries of the South and North, great disk going around heaven, earth, underworld, waters, and mountains, the great god, lord of Abaton, lord of all valor and victory given to him on the throne of Horus, pre-eminent of the living for ever."

Of greater interest are three Greek inscriptions on the bases of the obelisks. The first is a complaint by the priests of Philae addressed to Ptolemy IX, his sister, and his wife, which reads:

"Those travelers who visit Philae, generals and inspectors,

rulers in the Thebaid, and royal officials, scribes, and the chief-officers of the police, and all other officers who are in the service of the government, and the armed guards who are in the following, and the rest of their servants, compel us to pay the expenses of their maintenance while they are here, and by reason of this practice the temple is becoming very poor and we are in danger of coming to possess nothing. . . . We beseech you, O great gods, if it please you, that you give command not to annoy us with these vexations . . . to give us a written decision."

The second inscription is a copy of a letter from the king, his wife, and his sister, granting to the priests all that they had asked, and the third is a copy of a letter sent to the local official to implement the orders: "It is good that you should make suitable arrangements that no one under any pretext whatsoever should cause the priests annoyance in respect of the matters they have set out in detail."

The ancient practices of Egypt are enduring. Until recent times, the mayors of villages throughout Egypt have frequently complained of impositions made by government officials. In order to lessen their burdens, these mayors opposed the making of roads unless the roads would bypass their villages entirely.

When the decipherment of hieroglyphs is discussed, it is generally assumed that the Rosetta Stone alone was the key, but this is not the case; the Bankes obelisks also played a part. The Rosetta Stone bears three copies of a single text composed in honor of Ptolemy V. Two are in the Egyptian language—one in hieroglyphics and the other in demotic script. The third is written in Greek. From these it was possible to identify the hieroglyphic form of the name Ptolemy. Soon after his discovery of the obelisks on Philae, Bankes sent copies of the Greek and Egyptian texts to various scholars, pointing out the hieroglyphic form of the name Cleopatra which was until then unknown. The addition of this and the names of Alexander the Great and Berenice which were known from other monuments made it possible to isolate seventeen of the twenty-five letters of the hi-

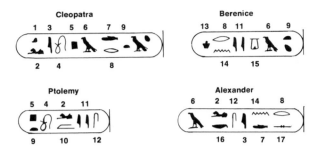

FIGURE 32. Key to hieroglyphs:
1= k, 2= l, 3= i, 4= o, 5= p, 6= a, 7= d, 8= r, 9= t, 10= m, 11= y,
12= s, 13= B, 14= n, 15= g, 16= k, 17= s

eroglyphic alphabet by comparing the hieroglyphic signs and their placement with the letters common to each name (fig. 32).

The fate of the cities which provided the first homes for the obelisks is sad indeed. The only monument that marks the site of Heliopolis is the obelisk of Sesostris I; the land around it is used as a soccer field by the neighborhood schoolboys. Piramesse has lost almost all of its monuments, and even the identification of its site is problematical. The fate of Memphis and Thebes is recorded in the Old Testament. Jeremiah prophesied that "Noph [Memphis] shall be waste and desolate, without an inhabitant" (Jeremiah 46:19). Nahum, when he threatened Nineveh, could find no better example of the fate of a great city than the fall of Thebes:

Art thou better than No-Amun [Thebes] that was situated among the rivers, that had the waters round about it, whose rampart was the sea? Ethiopia and Egypt were her strength, and it was infinite; Put and Lubim were thy helpers. Yet was she carried away, she went into captivity; her young children also were dashed in pieces at the top of all the streets; and they cast lots for her honorable men, and all her great men were bound in chains (Nahum 3:8–10).

CHAPTER SIX

Rome & Istanbul

THE epithets of Rome are numerous, yet one alone might better suit that metropolis than any other: the City of Obelisks (figs. 33, 34). While there are only eight obelisks standing elsewhere, Rome can boast thirteen, and more once existed there (plate 26). Among them is the largest obelisk now extant. All of them were brought from Egypt, although some were completed only after they arrived at Rome. Seven had been inscribed by pharaohs, two more by Roman emperors, one much later with a pseudo-Egyptian inscription; the rest have no inscriptions at all.[1]

Egypt was not altogether neglected at the beginning of the Roman occupation, although the country was regarded chiefly as a granary for Rome. The Romans were aware of the great civilization which had developed along the banks of the Nile. At the beginning of their rule, they were interested in the land and its continued prosperity. They erected temples and decorated some whose walls were still unfinished, all in the style of ancient Egypt. The figures of the emperors Augustus and Tiberius, dressed as pharaohs and with their names inscribed in cartouches, can still be seen depicted on the temple walls.

Toward the end of the pharaonic period, the Osirian triad, consisting of Osiris, the god of the dead, his consort Isis, and

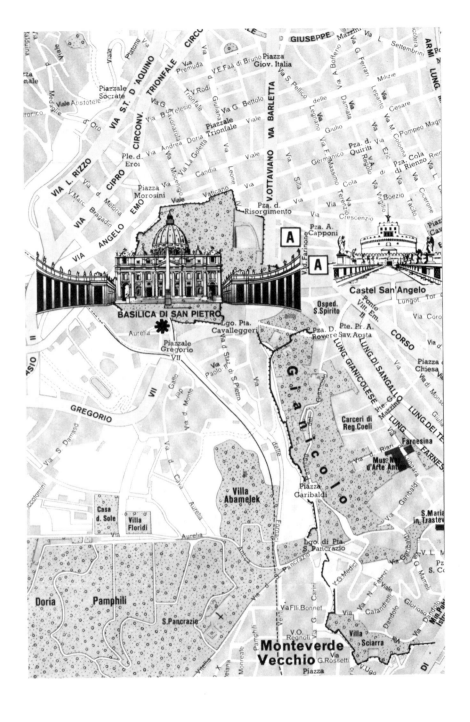

PLATE 26. Rome, with asterisks showing the approximate position of its obelisks

their son Horus, became predominant both in Egypt and throughout the classical world. For people who were suffering from bad economic and political conditions, Osiris offered hope of salvation. He typified good in contrast to evil, and his cult became increasingly popular. Along with his worship, that of Isis also spread abroad, for through her magic Osiris rose from the dead, and with her aid her son Horus avenged the death of his father.

After Egypt had been included in the Roman Empire, the cult of Isis spread throughout Europe. In many places the existence of shrines of that goddess has been revealed by the discovery of objects which originated in Egypt, and it seems likely that these objects were imported to add to the sanctity of the shrines. The cult of Isis may well have helped arouse the Romans' interest in obelisks.

The obelisk now in the Piazza San Giovanni in Laterano (more simply, the Lateran obelisk, the largest one now surviving) is made of red granite and was undoubtedly quarried in Aswan, perhaps from the quarry of the Unfinished Obelisk (plate 27). It is probable that Min, the mayor of Thinis and overseer of the priests of Onuris, was the man who supervised its construction for Tuthmosis III. Its present height is about 32.18 meters, a small part having been cut off when it was re-erected in the sixteenth century. Its weight is 455 tons.

The pyramidion of the obelisk is truncated. Both it and the upper part of the shaft were undoubtedly once plated with gold. On each face of the pyramidion the king is shown receiving the blessing of Amun-Re or Amun-Atum. On the upper part of the shaft, within a rectangular frame, the king is again shown making offerings to the gods. Below this, a column of inscription down the center of the shaft (plate 28) gives the names of Tuthmosis III, followed by phrases recording the obelisk's erection: "He [Tuthmosis III] made as his monument for his father Amun-Re, Lord of the Thrones of the Two Lands, the setting up for him of a single obelisk in the Upper Court of the Temple in the neighborhood of Karnak, on the very first occasion of setting up a single obelisk in Thebes."

PLATE 27
The obelisk in the Piazza San Giovanni in Laterano, Rome

PLATE 28
Inscriptions on two sides of the Lateran obelisk (after Marucchi)

Tuthmosis IV added a column of inscription on either side of the column carved for his grandfather. One line tells how the obelisk was left lying upon its side for thirty-five years in the hands of the craftsmen in the temple workshops. Another column describes how Tuthmosis IV embellished Karnak with several buildings, and still another states that he erected the obelisk at the Upper Gateway, opposite the city of Thebes.

Below these inscriptions of the third and fourth Tuthmosis, scenes were added by Ramesses II. Only those on the front of the obelisk survive; the corresponding scenes on the other faces were replaced at an unknown date with some unusual and non-Egyptian inscriptions.

The Lateran obelisk probably was extracted toward the end of the reign of Tuthmosis III. This late date is derived from two facts. After failing to extract from the Unfinished Obelisk a companion to the Lateran obelisk, Tuthmosis III did not have time before his death to order the completion of a mate. Also, according to the inscriptions added by Tuthmosis IV, the obelisk was not erected by his grandfather. This state of affairs would not have occurred unless the obelisk had been constructed close to the end of the reign.

Scholars have long been perplexed as to exactly where in Egypt the Lateran obelisk was erected. The French Egyptologist Gustave Lefebvre (1879–1957) examined its inscriptions and considered the possible places where it might have been erected in Karnak. Relying on the statements that it was destined for the Upper Court, or Gateway, of the temple, Lefebvre concluded that the obelisk must have been placed to the east of the main temple.[2] With this idea in mind, another French Egyptologist, Paul Barguet, searched for the exact site. Excavating to the east of the Festival Hall of Tuthmosis III, Barguet unearthed four huge sandstone blocks connected by dovetail joints. That these formed the base of the Lateran obelisk was confirmed by an adjacent scene added by Ramesses II in which the Upper Gateway is mentioned.[3]

Over a millennium after it had been erected, the story of the

Lateran obelisk was resumed. Ammianus Marcellinus wrote in the fourth century A.D. that he witnessed its erection in Rome. According to him, the obelisk was standing in Karnak when the emperor Augustus first considered taking it to Rome. Augustus seems to have changed his mind for fear that the obelisk's huge size would make it difficult to move and that its removal might anger the gods. About three centuries later, the emperor Constantine (A.D. 274–337) gave orders that the obelisk be removed from its original place. Because of the other monuments standing around it, it was evidently not easy to remove from the temple, and its pedestal and a large part of its foundation were destroyed. One of the blocks near the original site still plainly shows the marks made by the ropes used to lower the obelisk. At last it reached Alexandria safely and there awaited the building of a suitable ship to take it to Constantine's new capital at Constantinople.

The death of the emperor in 337 delayed the transport of the Lateran obelisk and ultimately changed its destination. Sometimes prior to 357, Constantius (A.D. 317–361), a son and successor of Constantine, ordered the obelisk to be taken to Rome. As reported by Ammianus, it was difficult to transport. A special barge was built, which carried the obelisk across the Mediterranean to the mouth of the Tiber and 3 miles up the river to the Villa of Severus. From there, the obelisk was removed to the Circus Maximus, where it was erected as a companion to an obelisk erected by Augustus many years before. On its top was placed a bronze orb covered with gold, but this was struck by lightning and was replaced by a bronze torch, also overlaid with gold and glowing like a flame. An inscription in Latin telling the history of the removal was engraved on the pedestal.

The obelisk was officially inaugurated during a short visit by Constantius in the spring of 357. It was the first great monument to be erected in Rome after the establishment of Christianity as the official religion, and for the Romans it symbolized the victory of the new religion over paganism. At an unknown date, perhaps several centuries later, the obelisk fell. Whether

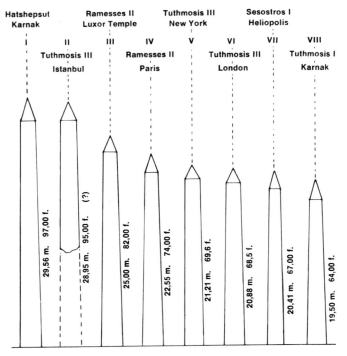

FIGURE 33. The standing obelisks outside of Rome compared

this was done by intent or happened through neglect is unknown, although the former alternative seems more probable. So huge a monument could not easily fall of its own accord.

The story of the re-erection of the Lateran obelisk comes from a sixteenth-century account by Monsignor Michele Mercati. He directed the attention of Pope Sixtus V to the existence of the obelisk and suggested that it be re-erected. Orders were given to search for the obelisk, and after several probings on the probable site, it was located some 7 meters below the surface in the marshy remains of the Circus Maximus. It was no easy task to remove the three fragments into which it had broken and to drag them through the narrow roads leading to its new site. This work and the subsequent erection took more than a year.

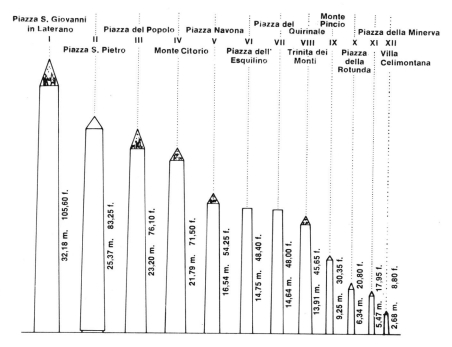

Piazza S. Giovanni in Laterano
I — 32.18 m. / 105.60 f.

Piazza S. Pietro
II — 25.37 m. / 83.25 f.

Piazza del Popolo
III — 23.20 m. / 76.10 f.

Monte Citorio
IV — 21.79 m. / 71.50 f.

Piazza Navona
V — 16.54 m. / 54.25 f.

Piazza dell' Esquilino
VI — 14.75 m. / 48.40 f.

Piazza del Quirinale
VII — 14.64 m. / 48.00 f.

Monte Pincio
VIII — 13.91 m. / 45.65 f.

Trinita dei Monti
IX — 9.25 m. / 30.35 f.

Piazza della Rotunda
X — 6.34 m. / 20.80 f.

Piazza della Minerva
XI — 5.47 m. / 17.95 f.

Villa Celimontana
XII — 2.68 m. / 8.80 f.

FIGURE 34. Twelve of Rome's thirteen obelisks compared

On August 3, 1588, the obelisk was finally in place in the Piazza San Giovanni in Laterano, resting on a new pedestal with four lions and scenes recounting its history. A cross was placed on its top. On August 10 of that same year, the consecration of the monument took place.

The obelisk in the Piazza del Popolo (plate 29) is the second most important obelisk in Rome. It is 32.77 meters high and weighs 235 tons. Three sides were decorated by Sethos I, but it was left to his son Ramesses II to decorate the fourth side. Ramesses also added two columns of text to each of the other sides already decorated by his father. Below scenes showing the kings making offerings to various solar deities there are numerous standardized inscriptions (plate 30). On one side Sethos I is

PLATE 29
The obelisk in the Piazza
del Popolo, Rome

PLATE 30
Inscriptions on two sides of the
Popolo obelisk (after Marucchi)

called "the one who fills Heliopolis with obelisks that their rays may illuminate the Temple of Re." On another side, Ramesses II is styled as "making monuments as innumerable as the stars of heaven. His works join the sky. When Re shines, he rejoices because of [the obelisks] in his temple of millions of years. His Majesty says, 'I beautify this monument for my father [Sethos I] to place his name in the Temple of Re.' " Indeed, Ramesses was responsible for the completion of the obelisk and for its erection in the sun temple of Heliopolis.

The Popolo obelisk was the first to be removed from Egypt to Rome. The feat of its removal during the first century B.C. was regarded with such admiration that the ship used to transport it was deemed worthy of being exhibited in Rome, only to be destroyed by fire some years later. In 10 B.C., the obelisk was set up on the *spina* of the Circus Maximus as a symbol of the sun and in commemoration of the conquest of Egypt by Augustus. Little else is known of its history during this period. It was still standing in the fourth century, and Ammianus gives a description of it in his account of the Lateran obelisk. He accompanied this description with a purported translation of the texts into Greek by an otherwise unknown Egyptian priest named Hermapion.

This obelisk too was lost sight of for more than a millennium. It was almost completely forgotten until one Alberti of Camaldoli found fragments of it in the ruins of the Circus. Under Pope Gregory XIII (1572–1585) sections of the base were also uncovered, but it was only in 1586, in the pontificate of Sixtus V, that an actual search for all of its parts was undertaken. After some time, it was decided that the obelisk should be re-erected in the Piazza del Popolo as a fitting centerpiece to a main approach to the city from which branches three of its principal avenues. A damaged section was removed from the bottom of the obelisk's shaft, and the original dedicatory inscription of Augustus was salvaged to be placed on a newly carved pedestal. The obelisk was re-erected in 1589.

The Piazza del Popolo has been subjected to many changes

since the obelisk was erected there. Pope Sixtus V himself planned to embellish the square further but he was unable to realize his ambitions. During the pontificate of Pius VI (1772–1799), plans to redesign the square were made. It was some time before they were carried out, but they resulted in its present form. The foundations of the obelisk were raised, and steps were added. The base was enclosed in marble, and around it were set figures of lions carved in the Egyptian style and spouting water into basins. Today the Piazza del Popolo is one of the most beautiful squares in Rome and one of the most beautiful settings for any obelisk removed from Egypt.

The obelisks of the Piazza della Rotunda (plate 31) and of the Villa Celimontana once formed a pair erected by Ramesses II at Heliopolis, and they were brought to Rome as a pair to be erected in the sacred enclosure of the Iseum, the Temple of Isis. That they were originally intended to be a pair can be deduced from their similar decoration and dimensions, despite the fact that both are now reduced in height.

The Rotunda obelisk is of red granite, 6.34 meters high. It lacks about a meter of its original height. On the pyramidion are the two cartouches of Ramesses II, and on each face of the shaft is the name of the king followed by a phrase expressing his relationship to the sun god: "Excellent son of Re, his sacred image, . . . protector of his creations who multiplies their offerings, . . . builder, great of monuments in the House of Re, . . . great of feasts like Re on the seat of Atum." Such phrases make it clear that this obelisk and its mate once stood in the Temple of the Sun at Heliopolis.

It is not known for certain who was responsible for the removal of these two obelisks from Egypt, nor is it known exactly when they were re-discovered. What is certain is that the Rotunda obelisk once lay near the Church of Santa Maria sopra Minerva, which is built over the ruins of the Iseum. Some time later, it is said to have been seen near the small Church of San Mauto on the Via del Seminario, where it still stood on its pedestal, although some fragments, perhaps from the bottom of its

PLATE 31. The obelisk of the Piazza della Rotunda, Rome

shaft, lay beside it. There it remained until the time of Pope Clement XI (1700–1721), when, after some indecision, it was decided to erect it in the Piazza della Rotunda in front of the Pantheon. A new fountain with water-spouting dolphins was made to replace an earlier one and to serve as a base for the obelisk. The top of the pyramidion was decorated with a cross surmounting a star, while the base of the obelisk received dedicatory inscriptions and copies of the papal coat of arms.

The mate to the Rotunda obelisk is the only one in Rome which stands within the walls of a palace and not in a public square. It is pleasantly situated in the garden of the Villa Celimontana where it can be approached and admired without becoming endangered by the fearful traffic of Rome.

Only the upper part of the obelisk, some 2.68 meters high and bearing the names of Ramesses II, still survives. A fragment of the lower part, like the upper part, once lay in the ruins of the Iseum, but it is now lost. Only a copy made by an early epigrapher of the inscriptions on two of its sides is known; the inscriptions parallel those of the Rotunda obelisk.

The obelisk reappeared on the Capitoline Hill to the east of the steps leading to Santa Maria in Aracoeli. According to references in contemporary documents, this must have taken place in the fourteenth century. For a century it remained on the Capitoline, but later it fell and seems to have been taken elsewhere. On September 11, 1582, the obelisk was presented by the city of Rome to Ciriaco Mattei, a nobleman of the city and a collector of antiquities. It was placed behind Mattei's villa, the Villa Celimontana, in a hippodrome which he had planned, and inscriptions placed on its base recounted the story of its donation.

Mattei's heirs gave little care to the villa or its obelisk, and in time these deteriorated to an extent that the obelisk seemed about to fall. An unexpected event caused its rescue. Prince Manuel de Godoy, a former prime minister of Spain, accompanied Charles IV and his queen to Rome after their abdication during the Napoleonic wars. Godoy took up residence in the villa once owned by Mattei. Having adopted archaeology and gardening as hobbies and wishing to restore his villa, the prince ordered the obelisk to be shifted to the Grove of Muses in the villa's garden, where it remains to this day.

The obelisk in the Viale delle Terme di Diocleziano (plate 32) and its counterpart form another pair whose history parallels that of the Rotunda and Celimontana obelisks. The pair too was erected by Ramesses II at Heliopolis, and as a pair they were removed to Rome to stand in the Iseum. On the pyramidion of the Terme obelisk is a winged scarab with a sun disk and the two cartouches of Ramesses II. On each side of the shaft is a column of

PLATE 32. The obelisk of the Viale delle Terme di Diocleziano, Rome

inscription listing the names of the king and epithets styling him as beloved of one or another of the solar gods and mentioning his giving offerings in Heliopolis. The obelisk is of red granite and stands 9.25 meters high.

In 1870, soon after Rome became the capital of a united Italy, a commission was formed to direct systematic excavations in the capital. The commission chose as a promising site the area which once had been the Iseum, and the Terme obelisk again saw the light of day on June 20, 1883. Not twenty-four hours had passed after its discovery before it was recognized that the obelisk had been originally set up in Heliopolis by Ramesses II and that its counterpart had been discovered some time before in the general vicinity but was by then in Florence.

The Terme obelisk, which once had stood in an African province of the Roman Empire, was again to have its fate involved with a "Roman" empire in Africa. In 1885, only two years after the discovery, war broke out between Italy and the ancient kingdom of Ethiopia, and Italian troops invaded that country. Two years later, a detachment of 548 Italian soldiers was trapped in an ambush and all were killed. To pacify public sentiment in Italy, it was decided to erect this obelisk as a memorial to the fallen soldiers. It was raised in front of the main railway station on a marble base adorned with lions' heads of bronze and bronze tablets on which were written the names of the soldiers who had died. The dedication of the monument took place on June 5, 1887, in the presence of the king, the queen, and the nobility.

In 1924, the square in front of the railway station was remodeled, and the obelisk was moved to a garden south of the Viale della Terme where it still stands. In this new position, the obelisk became involved in a second conflict between Ethiopia and Italy. When the former country was invaded by Italy, an obelisk from one of its ancient capitals, Axum, was removed to Rome. A bronze representation of the Lion of Judah, the emblem of the Ethiopian monarchy, dedicated to the emperor Menelik II, (1889–1915) was also taken. As if to avenge the soldiers commemorated by the Terme obelisk, the Lion of Judah was placed at the foot of the obelisk and unveiled in a public ceremony on May 9, 1937. This patriotic gesture had a perplexing end. During the days which followed the liberation of Italy by Allied troops in World War II, the bronze Lion of Judah disappeared without a trace.

The companion to the Terme obelisk was to have a different fate. It is assumed that it shared much of the same history as its mate, traveling from Heliopolis to be set up in the Iseum. When it left the Iseum is unknown. By the seventeenth century, it had been transferred to the Roman villa of the Medici, the ruling princes of Florence, and in 1790 it was removed to the Boboli Gardens in Florence, where it still stands. A granite shaft some 4.87 meters high, this Florentine obelisk of Ramesses II bears the same type of decoration as its companion in Rome.

The obelisks of Monte Citorio and Piazza della Minerva (plates 33, 34) both date to the Twenty-sixth, or Saite, Dynasty, a dynasty to which belong many of the monuments taken from Egypt to Italy in antiquity. Many of these in fact came from the city of Sais. It is not known whether these were taken because Sais, which had ceased to be important, was near to Alexandria, the capital of Roman Egypt, or whether they had been transferred to Alexandria earlier to embellish that city before they were removed from Egypt.

Psammetikos II, the third king of the Saite dynasty, was responsible for first erecting the obelisk of Monte Citorio at its original site in Heliopolis. As it stands now, this red granite obelisk is 21.79 meters high, and it may once have been taller. On each side of its pyramidion is a winged scarab holding a sun disk, with scenes of the king in the form of a recumbent sphinx on the shaft below. Owing to the bad condition of the obelisk, a large part of the texts is lost, and what remains is only the standardized list of the king's name: "The Golden Horus, 'beautifying the Two Lands,' beloved of Atum, lord of Heliopolis; the King of Upper and Lower Egypt, Neferibre, beloved of Re-Harakhti; the son of his own body, who seizes the White

PLATE 33. The obelisk of Monte Citorio, Rome

PLATE 34. The obelisk of the Piazza della Minerva, Rome

Crown and who unites the Double Crown, Psammetikos, beloved of the Souls of Heliopolis. On the First [Jubilee]."

The final line on the preceding inscription is the most important because it probably refers to a first Jubilee. It may seem
strange that Psammetikos II, whose reign lasted only six years,
celebrated a Jubilee, but one king who reigned only three years
is known to have celebrated one. A possible explanation is that
these kings may have reckoned their jubilees from a point
sometime in the reigns of their predecessors.

It is not known whether the Monte Citorio obelisk was still
standing in Heliopolis at the time of its removal to Rome. When
Egypt was conquered by the Romans, many parts of Heliopolis
must already have fallen into ruin. Like the Popolo obelisk, this
one was transferred by Augustus and reached Rome in 10 B.C. It
was erected in the Campus Martius on a granite pedestal with
an inscription referring to that emperor. The obelisk was set in
a pavement marked out in stripes and decorated with mosaics
representing the winds and possibly the signs of the zodiac.
Thus the obelisk formed the indicator either of a giant solarium
indicating the daily change in the meridional shadow or of a
giant horologium indicating the varying lengths of the hours of
the day. The former alternative seems the more probable.

The obelisk seems to have remained standing for many centuries, only being overturned during the tenth or eleventh century. Because it had once served an astronomical purpose, it attracted a special interest. After a long search it was located, and
Sixtus V issued instructions for it to be re-erected in March of
1587. Owing to its bad condition, however, in that same month
it was reburied instead. Later, Pope Alexander VII (1655–1667)
planned to erect the obelisk, but he too was unable to realize his
project.

Through the efforts of Pope Benedict XIV (1740–1758), the
obelisk was again found and in April 1748 it was removed from
a square where it was surrounded by tumble-down houses.
This discovery was considered of such importance that a tablet
commemorating the event was affixed to one of the buildings

near the place where the obelisk was found. The excavations which recovered the obelisk were characterized by systematic work, with archaeological data carefully recorded, an unexpected development at that period.

However, it was not yet time for the obelisk to be re-erected. Its bad condition as a result of fire and other damage had made its re-erection rather a problem. It was necessary first to find red granite to restore the base and shaft of the obelisk—no easy task. The requisite stone was finally found and after much more than three years of hard work the obelisk and its base were set up at Monte Citorio, thanks finally to the enthusiasm of Pope Pius VI. On June 14, 1792, a Latin inscription was added, telling the story of the obelisk's discovery and mentioning the people who took part in it, including the architect Antinori who was intrusted with the re-erection of the obelisk. It is curious that the only name of an architect which was preserved upon an obelisk whose erection he supervised was that of a man whose work did not prove permanent. Several years ago, the Monte Citorio obelisk was in danger of collapse; the blocks used in restoring the shaft had shifted from their original positions. In 1965, these blocks were put back in position, and with this restoration the obelisk is again safe.

The obelisk of the Piazza della Minerva was originally erected by the pharaoh Apries, the son and successor of Psammetikos II, who was known in the Bible as Hophra. His obelisk is of red granite and is 5.47 meters in height. The pyramidion is blank, and on each side of the shaft there is a single column of inscription, each beginning with the name of the king and followed by epithets naming Atum of the Land of Life, the cemetery of Sais; and Neit, She of the Bee-Temple in Mehnet, foremost of the Land of Life. These are deities connected with places at Sais.

Nothing is known of how or when the obelisk reached Rome. There is no doubt, however, that it was placed in the Iseum. It fell there and remained buried until 1665, when it was unearthed by Dominican friars who were laying a foundation for a new wall around the gardens of their church. This happened in the pontificate of Alexander VII, and the pope entrusted the antiquarian Athanasius Kircher (1602–1680) with supervising the clearance of the obelisk. It was soon decided to set it up in front of the church of Santa Maria sopra Minerva, quite near the site where it had first stood.

Many proposals were submitted for the design of the base of the Minerva obelisk, but in the end it was decided to place the obelisk on a statue of an elephant standing on a postament with four steps. On it were carved Latin inscriptions referring to the date of its erection, the pope responsible, and an injunction to people admiring the obelisk:

"Let any beholder of the carved images of the wisdom of Egypt on the obelisk carried by the elephant, the strongest of beasts, realize that it takes a robust mind to carry solid wisdom."

Alexander VII did not survive to witness the dedication of the obelisk, which took place on July 11, 1667, three weeks after his death.

The Minerva obelisk originally had a mate, but this has long since been broken into fragments, two of which were re-used to form parts of the obelisk at Urbino.[4]

The obelisks of the Piazza di San Pietro, Piazza dell' Esquilino, and the Piazza del Quirinale are all uninscribed. Their dates, provenances, and the reasons they were left uninscribed are not known. In his book on obelisks, the Danish Egyptologist Erik Iversen wrote, "There are certain indications that, at Heliopolis at any rate, uninscribed obelisks were still raised inside the local temple of the sun to serve as cult-objects, in the manner of their ancestors in the sun-temples of the 5th dynasty."[5] This may not be the case, however. Neither Flinders Petrie, nor any other excavator working in the ruins of Heliopolis, has ever found an obelisk, or even a small fragment of an obelisk, that was uninscribed. The sovereigns of ancient Egypt were ever eager to decorate monuments with their own names and with phrases proclaiming their own glory, no matter what the size of the monument. It seems strange that any of these kings would take the trouble of having such large obelisks fashioned, only to leave them undecorated. The only undecorated obelisks in Egypt were unfinished ones abandoned in their quarries, and in fact on one of these decoration was already in progress. More probably, the uninscribed obelisks were quarried in Egypt by the Roman emperors expressly to be taken to Rome, although it is possible that they were left incomplete because of the untimely death of a pharaoh.

The obelisk in the Piazza di San Pietro is important chiefly by virtue of its surroundings. It is made of red granite and stands 25.37 meters high. It was erected in the Julian Forum in Alexandria by order of Augustus and remained there until A.D. 37 when the Emperor Caligula ordered the forum demolished and the obelisk transferred to Rome. It was then erected in the Vatican Circus, and there it remained until its removal to the square before the Basilica of St. Peter. Legend has it that in the Vatican Circus innumerable Christians, including St. Peter, were put to death and that the reason this obelisk was not later overturned as were all the others in Rome was that it was looked upon as the last witness to the martyrdom of St. Peter.

From the mid-fifteenth century, popes had considered moving the obelisk from the circus to the Piazza di San Pietro, but owing to conflicts among the architects and to financial difficulties nothing was done. Sixtus V finally was able to have the obelisk moved to its present location (plate 35). Soon after his election, Sixtus V appointed a committee to choose the architect to whom the work would be entrusted. The pope did not approve of their selection, so he appointed as engineer Domenico Fontana (1543–1607), a man in whom he had every confidence. Fontana set to work immediately clearing around the obelisk, which stood deep in debris, and preparing the square for its reception. Scaffolding was soon erected around the obelisk, and the metal globe on its top, believed to contain the remains of Caesar, was brought down to be examined. (Nothing was found inside except dust.)

April 28, 1586, was fixed as the date for placing the obelisk on

PLATE 35. Fresco from the Vatican Library, showing the remo

he obelisk of the Piazza di San Pietro from the Circus Vaticanus

a cradle on which it would be taken to its new site. This was the first operation involving the obelisk itself, and Fontana, being a good Christian, attended mass with his men at two o'clock in the morning and later offered public prayers on the site to insure success. The work was accomplished, but not without difficulty. The obelisk had rested on four bronze crabs. Two of them were loose, but the other two were fixed firmly to both the pedestal and the obelisk by dovetails. Before the obelisk could be moved, the crabs, each of which weighed 600 kilograms, had to be separated from the pedestal, and this could be done only by chipping away the stone around them.

The obelisk was to be lowered from its pedestal and placed on the ground on May 9, 1586. On that day crowds from all parts of Rome were present to watch the work. Amid the applause of the populace, Fontana successfully performed the operation. The crowd could not contain itself, and Fontana was carried to his home to the accompaniment of drums and trumpets.

Fontana determined to re-use the bronze crabs and the old pedestal to support the obelisk in its new location, and he was able to remove them to the square. On June 13 the obelisk was also dragged to the square, and on August 30 the square was closed to the public in anticipation of the final stages of the work. On September 10 the obelisk was successfully brought above its pedestal, and on the 14th the cradle around it was removed. The obelisk again rested upon the four crabs, although these were now hidden by four double-bodied lions set at the corners of the obelisk.

For his success, Fontana was presented with the Golden Spur and a golden portrait medallion with heavy chain, a large pension, certain other prerogatives, and all the materials used in the transport of the obelisk. Indeed, the successful work of Fontana in so short a time was the subject of general admiration.

The dedication ceremonies took place on September 26, 1586. A mass was held in one of the neighboring churches and attended by many people including the papal court. A procession of all those attending the mass proceeded to the obelisk. There more prayers were offered; the obelisk was purified, and it was surmounted with a cross. This act was marked by a Latin inscription engraved on the top of the obelisk, referring to Augustus and Tiberius as the emperors who first removed the obelisk and to Sixtus V as the pope who re-erected it. The scaffolding was taken off, and the obelisk was enclosed by a stone railing to protect it from traffic. So it remains to this day.

The obelisk in the Piazza di San Pietro (plate 36) stands in the center of a square embraced by the majestic colonnades of the Basilica of St. Peter. It has witnessed multitudes of pilgrims who have come to worship there. More than once, I have seen the square completely filled with people from every part of the world, some so filled with emotion that they kneel in prayer on the rough pavement of the square. It is truly an inspiring setting.

The obelisks of the Piazza dell'Esquilino and the Piazza del Quirinale are both of granite, about 14.7 meters high. They seem to have been brought from Egypt at the same time to be used in Rome as a pair. In the sixteenth century, the two obelisks were lying near the ruins of the Mausoleum of Augustus. Since there is no mention of them in the description of this building when it was built in the first half of the first century A.D., and since they must have been erected at the mausoleum before it was abandoned as an imperial burial place at the end of that century, these obelisks must have been placed there in the second half of the first century.

According to Ammianus, the obelisks were still standing at the mausoleum in the fourth century, but by then their pyramidions had been removed. It is natural to believe that the two obelisks adorned the entrance of the building, but no trace of their base has ever been found. At some point, both obelisks fell, each breaking into three fragments. In 1519, the fragments of one were excavated and removed to a neighboring street. While many popes had intended to re-erect this obelisk, again it was Sixtus V who accomplished this. He gave orders to Fontana to make preparations for its erection, even though the latter was

PLATE 36. The obelisk of San Pietro, surrounded by a crowd listening to a papal message

already involved in the removal of the obelisk of San Pietro. Sixtus became so anxious that, since Fontana was occupied elsewhere, he named one Bandino de Stabia to transfer the three fragments to the square behind the Basilica of Santa Maria Maggiore, in front of the gate leading to the popes' summer residence on the Esquiline Hill. Fontana, when he had finished with his other tasks, turned his attention to this obelisk and was able to raise it in quite a short time. On March 11, 1587, excavations were effected in the place where the obelisk was to stand, and by the following August, the obelisk was set up. On August 11, the cross was affixed to its top, and two days later, it was dedicated.

The pedestal of the Esquiline obelisk was adorned with the usual dedicatory inscriptions. One is unique: it states that the emperor Augustus adored Jesus Christ as being born of the Virgin and refused to let himself be called "Lord" out of respect for the *Lord* Jesus Christ!

Sixtus V's ambitious plans were also extended to the Piazza del Quirinale (plate 37). He had this square redesigned to facilitate access to the Quirinale Palace, which was used at that time as a summer residence for the popes. (In 1870, it was seized by the government of the new united Italy to become the official residence of its head of state.) Fontana was again involved, and this time he transferred a pair of statues known as the "horse tamers" to the Piazza del Quirinale, repairing the parts of the statues that were badly damaged.

Almost two centuries later, in 1781, the companion of the Esquiline obelisk was unearthed, perhaps during the laying of foundations in the vicinity of the Mausoleum of Augustus. Like its mate, it was found in three pieces and was removed to storage in a neighboring street. Soon afterward Pope Pius VI decided to erect this obelisk between the horse tamers in the Piazza del Quirinale, but the project was to take almost five years. On January 14, 1782, a contract was let to the architect Antinori, who re-erected the Monte Citorio obelisk, to repair the obelisk, convey it to its new site, and erect it. There was much delay,

PLATE 37. The obelisk of the Piazza del Quirinale, Rome

and the three fragments were not placed on their pedestal until October 3, 1786. The dedicatory inscription told how the obelisk had been quarried in Egypt, taken to Rome to adorn the tomb of Augustus, and re-erected by Pius VI after having fallen to the ground. On October 21, the obelisk was formally consecrated.

The position of the obelisk was at first bitterly criticized, but soon it came to be greatly admired. Some thirty-two years later, a large basin was placed below the obelisk and the horse tamers, the combination of the three monuments making the setting of the obelisk unique, even for Rome, where no two obelisks have the same setting.

Like the San Pietro, Esquiline, and Quirinale obelisks, those of Trinita dei Monti, the Piazza Navona, and Monte Pincio, were uninscribed when they were brought from Egypt and may also have been quarried at the express order of the emperors. In Rome, however, the latter three were decorated with hieroglyphs; the first case with a copy of an ancient Egyptian inscription, and the other two with new texts written in the ancient Egyptian script in honor of the emperors who had ordered the obelisks.

The obelisk of Trinita dei Monti is made of red granite, 13.92 meters high, and stands at the top of the Spanish Steps. It is decorated with a copy of the inscriptions of Sethos I and Ramesses II on the obelisk in the Piazza del Popolo. In his detailed description of the obelisk of Trinita dei Monti, Iversen wrote that "judging from the poor workmanship of its hieroglyphic inscription Zoëga [the early Egyptologist Georg Zoëga, 1755–1809] assessed the time of its transportation to Rome to the period between Commodus (192) and Gallenus (268), a dating supported by its inscription, which is a late Roman copy of the Augustan obelisk, now standing in the Piazza del Popolo, as well as by modern archeological evidence." [6] Iversen pointed out that the foundations on which the obelisk was first erected were deeper than those of many of the surrounding buildings, placing its erection in about the third century A.D.

In ancient Egypt many monuments were inscribed with copies of reliefs taken from earlier periods, and other monuments were replicas of earlier constructions. In such cases, however, the author of the new monument never failed to substitute his own name for that of his predecessor. The mere fact that the text on this obelisk is a copy shows an interest in history. Without going into the details of Iversen's arguments, it seems possible that its unusual decoration might have been ordered by an emperor with an interest in history, and especially Egyptian history, such as the emperor Hadrian (A.D. 76–138).

In the fourth century, Ammianus wrote in his history that this obelisk, like those of the Mausoleum of Augustus, was brought to Rome after the death of Augustus, but he gave no indication as to which emperor ordered the work. What is known is that the obelisk was ultimately erected in the Gardens of Sallust, where its foundations are still to be seen. After the death of the owners, the gardens became imperial property. At some point the obelisk fell, but it was never completely lost.

Sixtus V reportedly thought of erecting the obelisk in front of the Church of Santa Maria degli Angeli, but this was never accomplished. Athanasius Kircher, who was the first to point out that the inscription was a copy of that on the Popolo obelisk, revived the idea of its re-erection to Alexander VII a century later, but to no avail. In 1734, during the pontificate of Clement XII (1730–1740), the obelisk was transferred to the Piazza di San Giovanni, but there it was to lie for fifty-five years. Sometime during that period there were abortive negotiations for taking the obelisk to Paris, where it would have stood in front of the Cathedral of Notre Dame. At last, Pius VI was able to bring the history of the obelisk to a happy conclusion. This pope decided to set it up in front of the Church of Trinita dei Monti, despite many protests. It was said that the foundations of the obelisk might endanger the church and the surrounding buildings and that its erection above the Spanish Steps might ruin the view. Such fears proved unfounded. When the obelisk was finally placed on its pedestal nothing happened, and indeed, the obelisk seemed a jewel in a splendid setting.

The story of this obelisk does not end here. Its base was finally unearthed in 1843, when an attempt was made to plant a tree in the gardens where the obelisk had stood so many centuries before. The base was removed and set up almost opposite the Villa Ludovisi, and there it remained until 1926. At that time, it was decided to use the base as a memorial to the fascist March on Rome of October 22, 1922. The base was appropriately decorated, and on October 28, 1926, it was dedicated at a new site on the Capitoline Hill.

The obelisk of the Piazza Navona (plate 38) is also made of granite, some 16.54 meters high. According to Iversen, it once stood between the Serapeum (the temple of the Greco-Egyptian god Serapis) and the Iseum in ancient Rome, but from its decoration it seems to have been more closely connected with the latter building. The emperor Domitian (A.D. 51–96) ordered this obelisk to be extracted from the quarries in the Aswan area, and a temple built there by Domitian may well date from the time when this was done. The obelisk is carved with hieroglyphs naming the Roman emperor.

Domitian did not follow the traditional pattern used in decorating the pyramidion. While the ancient pharaohs once showed themselves giving offerings to a single deity or receiving the god's blessing, Domitian showed himself between a pair of gods who gave him their benedictions or presented him with divine symbols. Iversen described these deities as "goddesses, reduced to subsidiary characters and adoring the king-god," [7] but this may be an overstatement.

From the scene in which a goddess, either Hathor or Isis, presents the Double Crown to the emperor, it seems certain that the obelisk was intended for the accession of Domitian in A.D. 81. This assumption is strengthened by the inscription on the shaft. There mention is made of Domitian's taking over from his elder brother Titus (A.D. 39–81) the empire left by his father Vespasian (A.D. 9–79) when the soul of Titus had "flown to heaven."

The obelisk of Domitian stood near the Iseum for some two

centuries, until Maxentius (emperor A.D. 306–312) transferred it to the circus which he erected in memory of his deified son Romulus (died A.D. 310). The remains of the circus can still be seen along the Appian Way. Again it is not known when the obelisk fell.

Although this obelisk was brought to the attention of Sixtus V, that pope was too busy with what he considered more important obelisks. Its erection was left to Pope Innocent X (A.D. 1644–1655). The Piazza Navona was chosen to be the new site. While still a cardinal, Innocent had occupied a modest building on the square. When he was chosen pope, he determined to mark this building by the erection of an obelisk in the adjacent square. The pope entrusted the work to the architect Girolamo Rainaldi (1570–1655), ignoring the distinguished architect Giovanni Lorenzo Bernini (1598–1680) who had been the favorite of Innocent's predecessor.

Bernini, however, had a plan for setting the obelisk above a fountain in the middle of the square, and he soon found a way to attract the attention of the pope. On the advice of a friend, Bernini made a model of his project, and the friend persuaded Olympia Maidalchini, the widow of the pope's brother, to place it in her house, where the pope visited from time to time. On one of Innocent's visits to his sister-in-law, his eyes fell upon the model, and he became so fascinated by it that he ordered Bernini to come to him immediately. The appointment of Bernini to the project was made on April 11, 1647, and in the summer of the following year, the obelisk was transported to the Piazza Navona. The pieces of the obelisk were not assembled until the year following that, and the entire fountain was not completed until the spring of 1651.

No cross was placed atop the obelisk but rather a dove, the heraldic symbol of the pope's family. The inscriptions on the pedestal told of this and of the particulars concerning the reerection of the obelisk; it also explained the meaning of the fountain below the obelisk. Bernini had made this foundation as an allegory of the four continents: Asia, Africa, Europe, and

PLATE 38. The obelisk of the Piazza Navona, Rome

America. He formed a series of caves in which were shown the representatives of the continents. The Ganges River, standing for Asia, was shown as a reclining river god with an oar in his hand. Africa was represented by the Nile, shown as a god with a hidden face, a gesture perhaps symbolic of the mystery of the Nile's source. Europe was shown by the mythical horse of the Danube, while America was represented by an American Indian awestricken by the obelisk. Other figures and animals peculiar to each of the continents were also added to the composition.

So great a work as Bernini's creation in the Piazza Navona ought to have been a great marvel to the inhabitants of Rome, but, on the contrary, there was much opposition to it. The high cost of the obelisk caused taxes to be raised, and this resulted in loud protests against the pope and his family. All this is now forgotten, and the obelisk and its wonderful fountain are the source of endless admiration.

The last of the thirteen obelisks standing in Rome is that of Monte Pincio; it is of granite, 9.25 meters high. Like the obelisk of the Piazza Navona, it was brought from Egypt by a Roman emperor to commemorate an important event. While Domitian had engraved his obelisk to mark his own coronation, the Monte Pincio obelisk was engraved by an emperor in the memory of a friend. Hadrian, who was responsible for the obelisk, took much interest in Egypt and its monuments; he even collected many of them for his villa at Tivoli outside Rome. During a trip which Hadrian made to Egypt, his friend and companion Antinous was drowned in the Nile under circumstances which are still not clearly known. Soon afterward, Antinous was deified, and in both Egypt and Rome temples were erected in his honor. In Egypt, even a town was named for him: Antinoupolis, the city of Antinous, opposite Ashmunein in Middle Egypt. In Rome, a mortuary temple was built for him and the obelisk was erected there. According to Iversen, this temple was annexed to that of the goddess Tyche-Romana, but its location is not yet known.

In the third century A.D. the obelisk was removed to the

Circus Varianus to decorate the *spina;* and at a date now lost, it fell. Its whereabouts continued to be known. The obelisk was appropriated by several private persons and traveled to various locations until it was finally acquired by Pope Clement XIV (1769–1772), who had it set up in the Vatican. Finally, in September 1822, the obelisk was removed to its present site in the Viale del Obelisco, by the order of Pope Pius VII (1800–1823).

Among all the obelisks removed from Egypt in the early centuries of the Christian era, the one in the Hippodrome in Constantinople (now Atmeidan, or the "Square of Horses", in modern Istanbul) was the last to be taken (plate 39). Unlike those brought to Rome, which suffered varying fortunes and were moved about that city, the Hippodrome obelisk seems to have remained standing in the place where it was set up after its removal from Egypt.[8]

The Hippodrome obelisk is one of a pair erected in the Great Temple at Karnak by Tuthmosis III and is probably shown in an offering scene of that king in the temple (fig. 35). The obelisk is made of red granite. Its present height is 19.8 meters, but an unknown portion of its lower half is missing. Where and when this part became detached cannot be said with certainty, and no fragment has ever been recovered. It is reported that the lower part also once stood in Istanbul, and the obelisk may have been broken after its arrival in that city. The beginning of the text on one of the obelisks shown in an offering scene of Tuthmosis III [9] corresponds to that of the Istanbul obelisk, and it shows that about one-third of the original obelisk may now be lost. It must once have been over 30 meters high.

The pyramidion of the obelisk is deformed, and the four sides of the shaft vary in width. On each of the faces of the pyramidion is shown a standing god holding the hand of the king and extending to him the sign of life. On the top of each face of the shaft is a scene of Tuthmosis III making offerings to the god Amun-Re, and, below the scene is a single column of inscription. Each of these begins with an elaborate list of the king's

PLATE 40
The front of the Istanbul obelisk with
its dedicatory inscription, cf. fig. 35

titles. Two of the texts continue: "Crossing the Great Circle of Naharina in valor and victory at the head of his army, making great slaughter . . . , Lord of Victory who subdues all lands, establishing his frontier at the Beginning of the Earth [the extreme south] up to the Swampy Lands of Naharina [the farthest north]. . . ." These remarks commemorate one of the most significant military victories of Tuthmosis III, the successful crossing of the Euphrates River in Syria.

An epithet of Tuthmosis III as Lord of Jubilees, is also given, and the obelisk may originally have been raised in celebration of such a festival. It is not known precisely which celebration was intended.

The chance preservation of a picture of this obelisk makes it possible to restore the complete text on the front of the obelisk (plate 40): "He made as his monument for his father Amun-Re, Lord of the Thrones of the Two Lands, the erecting [for him of great obelisks of red granite, the pyramidions being of electrum, that he—Tuthmosis II—may be given life like Re forever.]"

On the picture the names and figures of Amun-Re are erased, as they are on the surviving obelisks and fragments of Tuthmosis III at Karnak. On the Istanbul obelisk, however, these are untouched. This sug-

gests that the obelisk may have already been lying on the ground by the time the name of Amun-Re was destroyed by the followers of Akhenaten. This hypothesis seems to gain support from the fact that no successor of Tuthmosis III added any inscriptions to the obelisk. Ramesses II probably would not have resisted the temptation to inscribe his name if he had had the opportunity. He certainly did so on the Lateran obelisk of Tuthmosis III and the two obelisks of that king now in London and New York.

The Istanbul obelisk once stood to the south of the Seventh Pylon on that transverse axis of the Great Temple at Karnak. Recently the Franco-Egyptian Center in Karnak found ramps used in lowering this obelisk by the Romans. The direction of the hieroglyphs on the front of the obelisk indicates that it stood on the west side of the doorway. The lower part of the shaft of its companion still stands on its huge pedestal to the east of the doorway, while numerous fragments lie all around. The inscriptions on the surviving fragments show that this obelisk matched the one in Istanbul.

It is not certain who first started the latter obelisk on its journey to Istanbul. Constantine had the Lateran obelisk removed to Alexandria in preparation for its being shipped to Con-

FIGURE 35. Obelisks of Tuthmosis III as pictured in his temple

stantinople. After his death, Constantius shipped that obelisk to Rome. It is possible that in his turn Constantius caused the Istanbul obelisk to be removed to Alexandria for shipment to its present home. A letter from the emperor Julian (332–363) asked the Alexandrians to send to Constantinople the granite obelisk then lying in their city, for the transfer of which to Constantinople Constantius had had a freighter constructed. Obviously, Constantius's plan had not been carried out. Julian promised Alexandria a statue of himself in return for the obelisk.

There is no evidence that the Alexandrians heeded Julian's request, although it is possible. The inscriptions now on the base of the obelisk say only that prior to its being set up, it had lain for some time on the ground. The successful raising of the obelisk was credited to the emperor Theodosius (347–395) and to Proclus, his governor at Constantinople, who was entrusted with the actual work.

The pedestal which bears the inscriptions is divided into two sections (plates 41, 42). The lower part preserves inscriptions and two scenes showing the obelisk. In one, it is seen still resting on its barge, while in the other it stands on the *spina* of the Hippodrome, watching over a chariot race. The upper part of the pedestal shows the emperor and his court, in all probability as spectators at the chariot races in the circus around the obelisk.

The history of this obelisk presents more problems than that of many others. It was erected by Tuthmosis III, and some eighteen centuries later it was in Alexandria, but the date at which it fell and the circumstances of its survival are matters of conjecture. It was apparently taken to Alexandria only in order to be transferred to Constantinople. There, set up in the Hippodrome, the obelisk witnessed the chariot races and the strife-torn political life of the city. Near the obelisk were erected some of the greatest churches of Christendom, and for a thousand years all this endured. Then the races stopped; the empire decayed. The Ottoman sultans replaced the Christian emperors and the churches were converted into mosques. The obelisk remained to witness the growth of this center of the Moslem world and its decline amid the harsh realities of modern times. Stripped of its political and religious importance, Istanbul is now more a tourist center, and one of its principal attractions is the mighty shaft raised by Tuthmosis III so many centuries ago.

CHAPTER SEVEN

Paris, London, & New York

UNTIL the beginning of the nineteenth century, Egypt and its monuments had attracted little attention in Europe. Most of the Egyptian monuments found outside Egypt had been removed during the civilizations of classical antiquity, often to adorn temples dedicated to the goddess Isis. It was only after Napoleon Bonaparte came to Egypt on his abortive military campaign (1798–1801), accompanied by a group of scholars, that Europe began to take an interest in Egypt, its past and its present. In their colossal work *Description de l'Egypte*, these scholars gave an accurate picture of the people of Egypt, their customs, dress, and beliefs, and of the major cities and towns. More important still, they gave a detailed description of the ancient monuments and their hieroglyphic inscriptions, although these savants did not know the meaning of a single word that they copied.

From such information, interest in Egypt and its glorious past was engendered throughout Europe, and as a result the major states began to acquire Egyptian artifacts for their own collections. Foreigners, especially those occupying diplomatic posts in Egypt, were soon engaged at most of the important sites, picking up objects of value even as they destroyed Egypt's monuments to obtain them. The local authorities raised no objection to this wholesale plunder.

The real concern with the remains of ancient Egypt actually began only after the French Egyptologist Jean-François Champollion (1790–1832) discovered the key to the hieroglyphic script by means of the Rosetta Stone. On September 22, 1822, this genius sent a letter to Monsieur Dacier, secretary of the French Academy, announcing the discovery that was to open a new page in the history of one of the oldest civilizations in the world.

With the increased interest in Egypt that resulted, the governments of both England and France decided that they should have one or more of its obelisks to decorate their respective capitals. It was not difficult for these countries to gain permission to remove the obelisks, for Mohammed Ali, the effective ruler of the country although legally only the viceroy of the Turkish sultan, clearly desired to satisfy their demands even if it meant stripping Egypt of nearly all its major remaining obelisks. Since the number of obelisks was limited, both England and France laid claim to the best, and sometimes their claims conflicted.

The two obelisks of Tuthmosis III at Alexandria were first offered, the standing one to France and the fallen one to England. Before either could be removed, France applied for the two obelisks standing before the Luxor Temple. This pair, however, had already been promised to England. With the subsequent approval of the British representative, the Luxor pair was ceded to France, and the obelisk of Hatshepsut standing in Karnak was offered to England instead.

Fortunately for Egypt, Britain and France were unable to accept all these generous offers. This was not because of a noble intention to leave the obelisks where they stood; rather it was due to the huge expense and trouble involved in removing even a single obelisk. Each country finally contented itself with carrying away the best or the most easily removable obelisk granted to it, graciously agreeing to leave the others in Egypt. If all the obelisks considered had been taken, only three major ones would have remained in Egypt, a figure which would have been reduced to two when an obelisk was granted to the United

PLATE 43. The obelisk of Ramesses II in the Place de la Concorde, Paris

States later in the nineteenth century. The obelisks now in Paris, London, and New York are the results of this diplomatic policy.

The obelisk now in Paris (plates 43, 44) was the first to leave Egypt in modern times.[1] Like its companion still in Luxor, it is a monolith of red granite. It is only 22.55 meters high, somewhat shorter than the Luxor obelisk, and it weighs 227 tons. The decoration on the pair is similar. The pyramidion is left blank, while on the top of each face of the shaft Ramesses II is shown making offerings to Amun-Re. Below each scene are three columns of inscription. These give the titles of the king and tell of his valor and his piety. By his own account, Ramesses II was indeed a great king: ". . . the divine seed of his father Amun, lord of the gods, who causes the Temple of the *Ba* to be rejoicing and the Ennead of the gods of the Temple of the Lord [at Heliopolis] to be in joy . . . the king, distinguished [?] of monuments, great of victory, the eldest son of Re on his throne . . . who exalts the Domain of Amun like the horizon of heaven with very great monuments of eternity. . . . So long as heaven exists, your monuments shall exist, and your name shall endure like the heaven."

The idea of taking an obelisk from Egypt to Paris has sometimes been attributed to Napoleon. This may be true, since his campaign provided the occasion for a systematic examination of the monuments of Egypt, in-

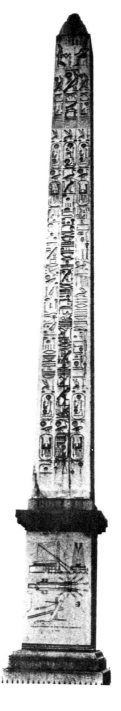

PLATE 44. The Paris obelisk

cluding the obelisks. It is reported that Josephine's parting words to her husband before he embarked for Egypt were, "Good-by! If you go to Thebes, do send me a little obelisk." [2] The actual events were less dramatic, yet it was this campaign which caused both England and France to desire obelisks; the English to commemorate their victory, the French to commemorate their scientific achievements.

After the restoration of the French monarchy in 1814, Louis XVIII decided to bring an obelisk from Egypt to adorn his capital. The king instructed his Consul-General in Alexandria to approach Mohammed Ali to see whether France could obtain one. The ruler of Egypt immediately offered the standing obelisk of Tuthmosis III at Alexandria, but little action was taken until Baron Isidore Taylor (1789–1879), a French writer of English ancestry and a well-known connoisseur and traveler, approached the French Minister of the Navy. Taylor intimated that only quick action on the part of the French would prevent the British from seizing the obelisk. Under such a threat, the question of removing the obelisk and getting it to France was again taken up.

Meanwhile Champollion, in a letter to the Minister of the Navy, pointed out that the poor obelisks of Alexandria were nothing compared to those of ancient Thebes and that if an obelisk were to be removed to Paris, it ought to be one of those in Luxor. The letter changed the plans already in existence, for the opinion of the decipherer of Egyptian hieroglyphs could not be easily dismissed.

Even before Mohammed Ali had approved the removal of an obelisk from Luxor, new plans began to emerge. There were many Frenchmen in the service of Egypt, and given Mohammed Ali's lack of interest in the history and monuments of the country and his eagerness to gratify all foreigners, it was taken for granted that no objection would be raised on his part. A committee was formed, headed by the Minister of the Navy, and proposals for the removal of the Luxor obelisks were submitted.

One major decision of this committee was to send Baron Taylor to Egypt to gain actual consent from Mohammed Ali for the release of the Luxor obelisks and also to acquire antiquities for the collection of the Louvre. In a letter dated November 25, 1829, the Minister of the Navy asked the new king, Charles X, for approval of the mission, and once this was granted, Taylor set forth, loaded with gifts for Mohammed Ali and his son Ibrahim Pasha, which were hoped to aid Taylor in his mission. Instructions were issued to the French consul-general in Alexandria to give every assistance.

The baron reached Alexandria on April 23, 1830, but was not granted an interview with Mohammed Ali until May 31. Meanwhile the two Luxor obelisks had been promised to the British. This did not deter Mohammed Ali, who arranged that they be given to the French and the British be offered the standing obelisk of Hatshepsut in Karnak as a substitute. The exchange was hardly a good bargain because of the difficulties that would have been involved in removing that obelisk.

The deteriorating relations between Egypt and France in 1830 did not affect Egypt's decision to give France the two obelisks from Luxor and the one standing in Alexandria, but it became imperative to hasten preparations for their removal. Since the end of June of that year, a transport had been waiting in Alexandria to move the obelisk from that city to France, and even before that, construction had begun in Toulon on a ship to be named *Louxor*, which would be capable of carrying the two Luxor obelisks down the Nile, across the seas, and up the Seine to Paris. Taylor was still determined to take all three obelisks to France, but the scheme was now beginning to be regarded as perhaps too ambitious and difficult to be carried out.

At this point, Champollion came forth with yet another suggestion. According to him, the obelisk standing to the west of the entrance of the Luxor Temple was the most beautiful of the three granted to France. It ought to be the first one removed. If time, interest, and money remained to remove the other obelisks, that could be done later. This advice proved sound.

Money was appropriated, and a naval engineer named Jean Baptiste Apollinaire Lebas (1797–1873) was appointed to direct the great operation of removing the obelisks from Luxor. Lebas was given orders to take the *Louxor,* which was scheduled for completion by the end of January 1831, from Toulon to Alexandria and then on to Luxor. There he was to examine the condition of the two obelisks and effect their removal. In case it proved impossible to transport both of them at once, the western one was to be removed first. Along with his orders, Lebas was given letters of introduction to people who might be of service to him and a copy of Champollion's report concerning the Luxor obelisks.

It was not until April 15, 1831, that Lebas was able to leave Toulon with the *Louxor,* but on May 3 he finally reached Alexandria where he docked opposite the palace. Owing to the absence of the French consul-general, Lebas's interview with the pasha was delayed for more than a month. Lebas was finally able to write: "At last on June 8 my interview with Mohammed Ali took place in the presence of the Consul-General. The governor, who knew beforehand of my short stature, pretended not to have seen me when I was presented to him by the Consul-General and asked, 'But where is your engineer? Tell him to sit beside me that I may be able to see him!' " [3] Indeed, the short stature of Lebas befitted his name, which means in French " 'the low one,' " and belied the high objectives which he was to accomplish. Lebas remarked that the interview was quite successful and that Mohammed Ali promised him all facilities, encouraging him in his great task and saying, "I am as much interested in it as if it were being executed in my own name and for my personal glory; the most strict orders have already been given that nothing which contributes to the accomplishment of this gigantic work is to be refused." [4]

It was then time to begin the voyage up the Nile. On June 11, 1831, the *Louxor,* accompanied by a number of local boats carrying necessary supplies, left for the mouth of the Rosetta Branch of the Nile, but low water delayed the voyage, and the ship did not reach Cairo until June 27. There Lebas's interview with Krali Bey, the director of navigation, caused him much worry. Krali Bey received Lebas in a tent beside the Nile and assured him that his task was impossible. Krali Bey said that even though Mohammed Ali had given Lebas permission to remove the obelisks, he would be unable to do so because of their huge size. What terrified Lebas was a statement that a large fissure began at the bottom and extended nearly one-third the way up the shaft of the western obelisk. This was indeed disconcerting news, and Lebas returned to his ship frightened and hoping that the director might be mistaken.

After much preparation at Cairo, Lebas finally proceeded upstream to Luxor on a journey filled with those adventures common to travelers in the nineteenth century. Arriving at Qena to the north of Luxor, Lebas was well received by the local *nazir*, or chief, in whose charge lay the town of Luxor. This official promised to provide him with anything he wanted, including many of the palm trunks so necessary for the successful completion of the work. When Lebas left the presence of the *nazir*, an unforeseen event took place, as he himself related:

"My surprise was extreme when I got out of his house, I was seized upon by the groom who perched me on a horse, whose enormous size contrasted in an unusual way with my small figure. My legs were almost horizontal. Since the position was extremely awkward, the chief of the grooms tried to convince me of the docility of the horse, by boasting that his master, aged and feeble though he was, could ride him while smoking his pipe. However, as a precaution he placed one of his men on each side of me to hold on to the bottom of my boots, and two others to hold on the tail of the horse and its bridle, while four men carrying torches went in front. In such a procession I was conducted to the ship. Once there, they gave me, as I expected, all signs of honor. For this I paid dearly, for one must tip all those who have shown such extreme signs of respect. In Egypt, as well as in other countries, those who are empty-handed are liable to be badly received." [5]

The next day Lebas reached ancient Thebes where he first visited the monuments on both sides of the Nile, and at last he landed at Luxor. The arrival there of the *Louxor* and its companion vessels must have attracted all the inhabitants of the region. When told of the reason for their arrival, the populace could not believe that it was simply to take away in one piece an obelisk from the temple. Their surprise was unbounded when Lebas was pointed out to them as the man who would remove the obelisk. One of them could not stop himself from saying: "Allah! Allah! . . . Who? . . . This man? But my stick is taller than he. . . . He is capable of stirring only the smallest stone from this temple!" [6]

When the crowd had dispersed, Lebas hurried to examine the western obelisk which had been the subject of some apprehension since his interview with Krali Bey. After sounding the stone, his Italian stone-cutter Mazacqui exclaimed, "Master, the stone is fissured but not broken through; we can remove it, but it has to be brought down slowly . . . very slowly." [7] He returned to the ship stunned that the fissure which had never been pointed out in any scientific book was known to Krali Bey. But Lebas was not a person to be discouraged by difficulties; on the contrary, they were a challenge to him. The next day, having had a good rest, he determined to go on with his work.

The appearance presented by the Temple of Luxor some 150 years ago was quite different from its appearance today. Houses had been built against the obelisks and the pylon, on top of more than 9 meters of debris which had accumulated over the ancient—and the modern—ground level. The interior of the temple was equally filled with debris on which rested still more houses and the Mosque of Abu el-Haggag (which still fills part of the first court of the temple), and small streets twisted through the tops of the temple's columns. Indeed, many parts of the temple were barely visible amid the later constructions which filled its entire length.

This situation both caused and solved problems. More than thirty houses stood around the obelisk and along the intended route by which it would be taken to the Nile. A committee had to be formed to negotiate with the owners of these houses so that they might be removed. After many conferences, a satisfactory agreement was finally reached.

It was equally important to find places to lodge the workmen and Lebas's staff and to keep safe the materials needed for the various removal operations. To find such buildings, Lebas had little choice: only the buildings which had been erected inside the temple itself could fill his needs, and Lebas was to make use of most of them. To the west of the temple, overlooking the Nile, was the house of the *Brin-bachi,* or governor of the town, and this Lebas chose as his own dwelling.

When all was organized, work began, albeit under rather difficult conditions, for it was summer and the temperature in Luxor could sometimes exceed 120 degrees Fahrenheit. First, houses were pulled down and earth was taken from one place to another according to need; carpenters surrounded the obelisk with scaffolding; sailors prepared planks to receive it aboard ship. Such activity had scarcely been seen in Luxor since the days of the pharaohs.

Problem after problem had to be faced. News reached Luxor that cholera was rampant in Lower Egypt, and many of the Europeans hurried to leave Luxor in order to escape this dread disease. When the epidemic reached Luxor, many people, including some working on the obelisk's removal, lost their lives. Owing to the dire situation within the country, materials ordered from Cairo did not arrive, and Lebas had to depend on whatever he could discover locally. With his own enthusiasm and the zeal of those working with him, he achieved, in his own words "the removal from the ancient capital of the civilized world of one of its most beautiful pieces of decoration." [8]

October 23 was fixed as the day to begin lowering the obelisk. One hundred and ninety workmen stood waiting in their proper places, and when the first rays of the sun fell upon the colossal statue of Ramesses II, the men began to act. Within twenty-five minutes, the obelisk had been inclined by some 25 degrees, but this rapid pace did not continue. Only on November 16 was the obelisk finally on the ground. It was then observed that Ramesses II had had his name engraved on the very bottom of the shaft, where it could be neither seen nor erased. Ramesses had usurped so many monuments of his predecessors, erasing their names and adding his own, that he knew well the need for this hidden inscription!

Once the obelisk was on the ground, it still had to be dragged to the ship *Louxor*. This took great effort, and not until December 19, 1831, was the obelisk safe on board. One can imagine the great joy and satisfaction of the participants now that this first part of the great enterprise had come to so successful an end. The inhabitants of Luxor, not believing that the removal could have taken place, went around the place where the obelisk once stood, saying, "This is the work of devils!" The red marks of Sherif Bey, the governor of Upper Egypt, who arrived at Luxor on the day after the embarkation of the obelisk, reflected a more educated view: "I did not believe that it would be possible to transfer on board a ship such a considerable weight. This enterprise seemed to me unfeasible, and I can assure you that I was not the only person in Egypt of that opinion." [9]

Lebas was not one to deny the magnitude of the task which he had just completed:

"After four and a half months of fears and worries the problem is solved! It required bringing more than ninety thousand cubic meters of sand, cutting through big mounds of earth, pulling down thirty houses, building more houses on the roof of the temple, and at last erecting the quarters necessary for lodging one hundred and forty men, and all that in a country which has no resources, in the middle of the sand of the desert, amidst the turbulent tortures of a boiling earth, and under a sun which makes the thermometer rise up to 50 degrees[C]." [10]

Before the next inundation of the Nile which would provide sufficient water to move the *Louxor* safely downstream, Lebas proceeded north to examine the situation in the Rosetta Branch of the river to see if his ship could be taken through the river's mouth into the Mediterranean. All conditions proved satisfactory, and he returned to Luxor to arrange for the departure of the obelisk. There, the *Louxor* was aground, but only awaiting the waters of the inundation to lift it off. On August 25, 1832, this happened. The ship left Luxor, went downriver, and finally reached Alexandria. After three months there, the *Louxor* left for France, landing at Toulon on May 11, 1833.

With the obelisk safely in France, Lebas considered his task completed, but it did not end at that point. He soon received a letter telling him that he was to erect the obelisk in Paris as well. "The cleverness of which you have given many proofs in bringing the monolith to the interior of France assures the complete success of the new operation which you are to take over." [11] With these encouraging words, Lebas went immediately to work. The center of the Place de la Concorde had been decided upon as the site, and preparations for raising the obelisk were begun there. Meanwhile aboard the *Louxor,* the obelisk was put on a cradle, and stone for the pavement and a pedestal were set on board. All were taken up the Seine to a point near the Place de la Concorde, arriving on December 15, 1832.

Work was soon completed on the pavement and the pedestal, and the obelisk was brought into position. On October 24, 1833, three hundred and fifty men of an artillery command were on hand to assist in the final stage of operations. At the blast of a trumpet, the machinery began to move, and the obelisk on its cradle was suspended in the air. At that moment, it would have been easy to complete the operation of erecting the obelisk, but orders postponed the event to the following day.

From early in the morning of October 25, more than 200,000 spectators began to fill the Place de la Concorde, the avenues branching out from it, and the terraces of the Tuileries. All Paris seemed to want to witness the completion of an enterprise which had begun more than three years before in the ruins of ancient Thebes.

At noon, the king and queen and the royal family took their

places on the balcony of the Ministry of the Navy overlooking the square, where they were greeted by the crowds. By that time the monolith had already reached an angle of 38 degrees, for work had started before their arrival. After three hours more, the obelisk was erect, amid the applause of the assembled crowd.

The ceremonies were crowned by a dinner given by the king on behalf of his faithful servants. Lebas was given silver and bronze copies of a medallion bearing the image of the king and having the following inscription: "Under the reign of Louis-Philippe I, King of France, M. de Gasparin being Minister of the Interior, the Obelisk of Luxor was raised by M. Apollinaire [Lebas], engineer of the Navy." There were copies of two other medals placed in a hollow in the pedestal below the obelisk. Lebas also received a large sum of money, and the people who had assisted him in his work were similarly rewarded.

The Paris obelisk now stands in the center of the Place de la Concorde, one of the largest and most beautiful squares in the world. Surrounded by fountains and overlooked by pavilions housing statues representing the great cities of France, the obelisk serves as a terminus to the Champs Elysées. The splendor of this square is such that the French can be forgiven for taking away one of the only pair of obelisks previously left standing in front of an Egyptian temple. Commenting on the missing obelisk my late friend, the artist and historian of Egyptology, Leslie Greener (died 1975), said of the Luxor Temple, "Its imposing pylon gate will always have the bereft appearance of an elephant with one tusk missing!" [12]

The obelisks of Tuthmosis III were once numerous, but none now stands in Egypt. The pioneer American Egyptologist James Henry Breasted wrote of them:

"Tuthmosis III erected a series of at least seven obelisks, of which five were in Thebes and two in Heliopolis. The latter now stand face to face on each side of the Atlantic, as they stood side by side at the portal of a Heliopolis temple. Of the five at

Thebes, not one survives in Egypt; all having perished save two and these are now in Europe, one in the Piazza of the Lateran in Rome, the other in Constantinople. We are thus presented with the surprising spectacle of the greatest of the pharaohs without a single surviving obelisk in the land he ruled while the modern world possesses a line of them reaching from Constantinople to New York." [13]

The two obelisks Tuthmosis erected at Heliopolis were the last colossal monuments to leave Egypt—one to grace the old world, the other to grace the new. The obelisks now in London and New York once formed this pair, and they are quite similar in size, description, and decoration. The London obelisk is of red granite, 20.87 meters high, and its weight is estimated at 187 tons. That of New York is also of red granite but is slightly higher and heavier than its mate, being 21.2 meters high and weighing about 193 tons.

The decoration of the pair follows a common pattern. On each side of each pyramidion, Tuthmosis III is shown as a sphinx making offerings to the gods of Heliopolis. On each face of each shaft are carved a central column of inscription by Tuthmosis III and subsidiary columns by Ramesses II on either side of it. These inscriptions follow the normal conventions, mentioning the piety and prowess of the kings. An inscription by Tuthmosis III on the London obelisk gives the reason for the pair's manufacture: "[Tuthmosis III] made as his monument for his father Re-Harakhti, the erecting for him of two large obelisks [with] pyramidions of electrum on the third occasion of the Jubilee through the greatness of his love for his father Atum." From the obelisk in New York it is known that the pyramidions were to "illuminate" Heliopolis, the city in which they were erected.

The London and New York obelisks originally stood in front of the Temple of the Sun in Heliopolis, and they seem to have been erected there by Yamunedjeh, the first herald of the king, for Tuthmosis III on the occasion of his Third Jubilee in his Year 37 (about 1468 B.C.). They remained at Heliopolis some fifteen

PLATE 45. "Cleopatra's Needle" on the Thames Embankment, London

centuries before they were taken to Alexandria. In the eighteenth year of the reign of the emperor Augustus (c. 10 B.C.) they were set up there by the prefect publius Rubrius Barbarus and the architect Pontius. They stood in front of the Caesarium, the temple of the deified Julius Caesar, resting upon bronze crabs, symbols of the Roman sun god. What was to become the London obelisk fell in an earthquake in 1301 A.D.; its mate remained standing until it was removed to New York.

Augustus had taken some interest in the gods of his new province of Egypt. In addition to erecting the obelisks at the Caesarium, he also built the temple at Kalabsha, called the "Karnak" of Nubia because of its vast size, and the elegant temple of Dendur. The latter has been awarded to the United States in gratitude for help in salvaging Nubian monuments threatened by the Aswan High Dam. Some day it will stand in New York less than 91.5 meters from the obelisk which Augustus moved to Alexandria.

It is strange that these two obelisks of Tuthmosis III should have acquired the name of "Cleopatra's Needles" (plate 45), for they were erected in Alexandria some twenty years after Cleopatra's death. It is conceivable that she may have caused them to be taken to that city and for some reason they were not erected. More probably, her name was merely attached to

PLATE 46. The London obelisk

them in a romantic fashion, just as there are in Alexandria, Mersa Matruh, and Aswan places called "the Baths of Cleopatra," although there is no evidence that the queen ever bathed there.

The story of the removal of one of the obelisks (plate 46) to London spans more than three quarters of a century.[14] It began after the French fleet was destroyed at the Battle of Abukir (July 25, 1799) and the French army was defeated at the Battle of Alexandria (March 21, 1801). The French were allowed to evacuate Egypt unhindered, but under the terms of the capitulation, as mentioned earlier, they were forced to hand over certain antiquities. The earl of Cavan, who had been in charge of a British regiment in Egypt, decided to leave a record of these victories and ordered a plaque engraved with an account of the Anglo-French conflict to be placed under the fallen obelisk of Tuthmosis III at Alexandria.

But Cavan's eye was on a more significant memorial for this campaign: the removal of the fallen obelisk to London. The Turks, then the official rulers of Egypt, looked with favor on the British victory and when approached by Cavan they immediately acceded to his request. The earl drew up plans and asked his troops, who were still in Egypt, to contribute to the expenses of the project by each giving up several days' pay apiece. This they did willingly, out of pride in having taken part in the victory. With money thus collected, work was started by building a jetty to assist in moving the obelisk toward a ship which would take it to England. The work was well advanced when it suddenly came to an end. The reason is unknown; some believe that orders were issued by higher naval authorities, while others hold that the cause was a heavy storm which washed away the jetty. In any case, the British army soon retired from Egypt, and the obelisk remained behind.

The actual removal of the obelisk did not occur for many years. In the interval, many attempts were made to arouse the interest of the people and government of England, but without success. Samuel Briggs, who had been the British consul in

Alexandria from 1803 to 1809, on returning to Egypt in 1820 on a personal visit, found the situation favorable for the removal of the obelisk. Mohammed Ali consented to release it and the intrepid Belzoni, who had moved the Philae obelisk to W. J. Bankes's estate in England, was ready to arrange its transport to England. Briggs wrote to one of the ministers of George IV outlining the situation, but although the king himself ordered that the letter be considered by the Foreign Office, Parliament did not approve the necessary funds. The obelisk moved no closer to England.

As if anxious to get rid of the obelisk, Mohammed Ali repeated his offer in 1831, even promising to move it at his own expense to the ship which would take it to England. This generous offer did not stir the authorities in Britain to action, nor did the rumors current in 1847 that the French had their eyes on the same obelisk. But certain people in England did become enthusiastic about the project. Among them was the politician and philosopher Joseph Hume (1775–1855). He unceasingly prodded the government, with the result that serious discussions were begun on the cost of moving the obelisk and the ways this might be accomplished. These were brought to an end by the protest of a group of distinguished archaeologists headed by the eminent Egyptologist Sir Gardner Wilkinson (1795–1875); the group considered that the obelisk was in such bad condition as to be unworthy of removal!

When plans were being made for the Great Exhibition of 1851 at the Crystal Palace in London, interest in the obelisk revived. The Crystal Palace Company, seeing that the government had failed to remove the obelisk in half a century, asked for permission to assume the responsibility of doing so. The offer was refused: it was considered essential that, if the obelisk were to be brought to England, it should be as a national monument and not as the property of a private company.

Finally, General James E. Alexander (1803–1885), a successful soldier who had written many books on his worldwide travels, took up the cause of the obelisk. Alexander was a man of strong character with an ability to influence people. Having visited Paris in 1867 and been fascinated by the obelisk in the Place de la Concorde, he wrote, "I now determined to endeavor to save the national disgrace of the loss and destruction of the trophy . . . the prostrate obelisk . . . and resolved to do my utmost to have it transported to London, to grace the metropolis with a monument similar to those of Rome, Paris and Constantinople." [15] Even with his abilities, this effort was to take almost ten years.

In spite of a lack of encouragement, General Alexander proceeded with his campaign, reading papers to scientific societies, showing the feasibility of bringing the obelisk to London, and arguing that the obelisk would add to the beauty of England and save the country's dignity. To learn what was needed to carry out the scheme, Alexander decided to go to Egypt to inspect the obelisk and to approach the authorities there for help in realizing his dream.

With a recommendation from the Foreign Office, Alexander contacted General Edward Stanton, the British agent and consul-general in Egypt, and with his help was given a special audience with the Khedive Ismail on March 25, 1875. He was royally received, being escorted by an officer to the presence of "a pleasant looking man in good condition, wearing the usual fez on his head, and dressed in dark surcoat and trousers and white vest. No signs of rank about his person, all perfectly plain." [16]

The General left a vivid description of the interview:

The Khedive, who spoke French, showed us the way to a handsome reception room, and bowed at the door for us to enter first. Of course we declined to do so. He then went to an upper corner, and we sat on either side of him on a divan. The Consul-General said that I was a zealous antiquary, and had come from England about the prostrate obelisk at Alexandria, to examine its condition, and ask permission for its removal from his Highness. He replied, "This obelisk was presented to the British Nation by my ancestor Mohammed Ali Pasha, for services rendered to Egypt; it belongs to Britain, I give it up freely. How is it to be removed?" [17]

Content with the success of his audience, the general responded by giving all the details of the plan by which the obelisk was to be removed to England.

At that time, Alexander made contact with an engineer named Waynman Dixon of the North England Company who agreed to work on the removal of the obelisk. Dixon cleared all around it to determine its condition, which proved to be satisfactory, and drew up a plan for its removal.

The next step was rather delicate, for it was to obtain the consent of the owner of the land on which the obelisk actually lay. He was a rich Greek merchant named Demetrio. General Alexander wrote:

"I visited Signor Demetrio twice, the second time in the company of Mrs. Gisborne. Female influence was of service and he gave full liberty to have the obelisk removed from his ground. Afterwards, a legal friend has persuaded him to demand a sum of the Egyptian Government for allowing his ground to be obstructed by the presence of the obelisk, but this difficulty Mr. John Dixon managed to overcome." [18] How Dixon did this is not known; perhaps it was managed "unofficially."

The official version was that Demetrio was hurt because the Egyptian government had given the obelisk without his approval, and that the difficulties were solved when a document was signed saying that the owner of the obelisk had given it as a gift to England. Unofficially, he seems to have made further demands. As a matter of fact, Demetrio had been imploring the Egyptian authorities to remove the obelisk from his land, but finding no response, he was about to cut it into pieces and use it as building material.[19] But once it was chosen to be sent to London, he pressed his claims for remuneration. Fortunately steps were already being taken to remove the obelisk from his grasp.

With the situation in Egypt in hand, General Alexander returned to England to submit his plans and to get money to carry them out. Among government authorities, he found little interest, the excuse always being the same: there is no money for such an ambitious scheme! He then turned to private resources where he found support in Sir Erasmus Wilson, an aging physician who had accumulated a goodly fortune. After a meeting between Wilson, Alexander, and Dixon, Wilson approved to such an extent that he agreed to provide £ 10,000 or more to have the obelisk brought to London and erected on the bank of the Thames. The contract was signed by the end of 1876.

In order to transport the obelisk, Dixon had a special barge designed. It was divided into ten watertight compartments and looked like an enormous boiler. This special construction was to prove farsighted. When the barge was completed in England, it was shipped to Alexandria in sections to be built around the obelisk.

Before the obelisk could be loaded into its barge, the whole area around it had to be cleared. During this work, many antiquities were discovered: lamps, amphora, even tombs with skeletons. Then houses and large stone blocks on the route to the sea were blasted away, and a channel was dug from the obelisk to deep water. On shore, the obelisk was placed inside its special barge, now called the *Cleopatra*, which was then towed to the harbor. Henry Carter was captain of the barge, and a crew of five sailors and a carpenter were engaged for it. Arrangements were made for the steamship *Olga* to tow the barge and its obelisk. On Friday, September 21, 1877, the *Olga*, towing the *Cleopatra*, set out on its voyage to England.

The trip was beset with difficulties from the start. First the heat was extreme; then came massive storms. Two of the crewmen of the *Cleopatra* were injured and had to be set ashore, and poor Captain Carter was left to carry on with the remaining crew. Serious trouble finally overtook the two ships in the Bay of Biscay on the evening of the 14th and the morning of the 15th of October. John Dixon summarized the tragedy:

"It seems that on Sunday evening the gale was so severe that the *Olga* cast off tow ropes, and about 10 o'clock a tremendous sea overwhelmed the *Cleopatra,* broke some of the rail ballast adrift and left her with a strong list to starboard. Captain Carter, fearing another such sea might capsize her, signalled for assistance. The *Olga* sent a boat with a volunteer crew, which found the *Cleopatra* and caught the ropes thrown to them, but could not hold on and drifted away. The *Olga* imagined her boat was with the *Cleopatra.* At daybreak, the gale continuing, a very skilful attempt was made to get the *Cleopatra's* crew on board of the *Olga.* This proved successful, and it was then found that the boat's crew were missing, and the *Olga* steamed away to look after them. The search proved fruitless, and on returning the *Cleopatra* could not be found, and the *Olga* at once headed for Falmouth." [20]

Dixon insisted that the *Cleopatra* with its precious cargo was still safe and that it would remain afloat until it was picked up by another ship, and he appealed to the First Lord of the Admiralty to send ships to seek it out and bring it to England. At the same time that Dixon's statement reached *The Times,* a telegram was received from a Lloyd's subagent in Ferrol, Spain, saying that the *Cleopatra* had been picked up by a Glasgow steamer, the *Fitzmaurice,* owned by a Mr. Burrell, and had been towed into Ferrol.

This news was received with great pleasure, but the loss of the boat's crew lay heavily on the conscience of England. Before the telegram could be confirmed, a message was sent to Dixon, saying, "The Queen heard with pleasure the recovery of the Needle and earnestly hopes the poor men were saved." When it became clear that there was no hope of their salvation, bitter recriminations were made over the timing of the voyage. It was known that storms were common in the Bay of Biscay at that time of the year, and a great storm had actually been expected to reach the bay at the very moment when *Olga* and *Cleopatra* were passing through it. Criticism after criticism was made of the planning of the voyage, but Dixon always managed to defend himself.

The widows of the lost seamen were each given a substantial sum of money, and at Queen Victoria's suggestion, it was decided to carve their names on the base of the obelisk. They had lost their lives in a valiant attempt to preserve the lives of *Cleopatra*'s crew and deserved to be commemorated. It is ironic to reflect how many in ancient Egypt lost their lives or were injured in moving the great obelisks. For them there was no memorial.

The saving of the *Cleopatra* was followed by still more unpleasantness. Burrell, the owner of the *Fitzmaurice*, demanded £5,000 salvage, a sum which surpassed any figure imagined by Dixon. Burrell was told that he should be content that his vessel had the honor of picking up the *Cleopatra*. Burrell refused an offer of £600, and is said to have finally accepted 2,000. When the *Cleopatra* was returned, almost everything aboard her had been "salvaged." Captain Carter lost his clothes, money, rare coins and jewelry, even his private letters. The mate of the *Fitzmaurice* was seen wearing the good captain's shirt studs!

On January 15, 1878, the ship *Anglia* began to tow the *Cleopatra* under the command of Captain Carter from Ferrol to England, and the ships reached Gravesend on the 21st. There they were met by General Alexander and John Dixon, with a telegram from the queen congratulating them on bringing the obelisk safely. With this the memorable voyage ended.

Long before the obelisk began its journey to England, a sometimes heated discussion about its proposed site had developed in letters sent to the *Times*. There was hardly a place of any importance in London that was not suggested for the obelisk: Parliament Square, the forecourt of the British Museum, St. James Park, Kensington Gardens, the Thames Embankment. One site after another was dropped, and finally the bank of the Thames was settled on. By erecting it there, the risk of destroying pipes, cellars, and roadways in the city was avoided.

On January 27, the *Cleopatra* was brought up the Thames and moored near the Houses of Parliament. All along the way, it was greeted by multitudes of people. At a meeting of the Metropolitan Board on February 15, 1878, it was decided that the obelisk should be erected on the Victoria Embankment. On May 30 the obelisk at last reached its final destination near the Adelphi Steps to await its erection.

The pedestal of the obelisk had been lying near it in Alexandria at the beginning of the nineteenth century, but by the time the obelisk was actually transferred to England, the pedestal was nowhere to be found. Possibly Mr. Demetrio broke it up for use in one of his buildings; in any case its fate is a mystery. Before the obelisk could be set up, a new base had to be fashioned. This was adorned with four bronze plaques recounting the obelisk's history and listing the persons associated with it during its many peregrinations.

September 13, 1878, was set as the day for the erection of the obelisk. This took place without any ceremony, but in spite of unpleasant weather, thousands of people gathered to see the obelisk being raised. When it stood in place, a correspondent of the *Times* reported:

"The enthusiasm of the crowd, as though the wonder they already saw before them had now for the first time struck them in all its grandeur, burst forth in ringing cheers, which were renewed from the river, road, terrace and bridge as the Union Jack was run up on the flagstaff which overtopped the pyramidion on the north side, and again the Egyptian [Turkish] flag followed on the south. These cheers for the colours were in honour of the Queen and the Khedive; but the first burst was for Dixon and his coadjutors, and in recognition of a great triumph already won." [21]

Of the principals who had worked so long to get the obelisk moved, only one name was omitted from the bronze plaques: that of General James Alexander. Of the final moments of the erection of the obelisk, the general commented, "I . . . viewed it from the deck, with considerable emotion, suspended in midair, whilst reflecting on all the anxiety and trouble, and expenditure of time and means it had occasioned, but extremely thankful withal to see at length the accomplishment of the dream of ten years." [22] He was satisfied that his dream was realized, whether or not his own role was acknowledged.

The story of the New York obelisk (plate 50) encompassed a much shorter period than that of its mate in London.[23] At the opening of the Suez Canal in 1869, the Khedive Ismail first offered an obelisk to the United States. This offer was not given much consideration until the removal of the fallen obelisk to London in 1877 aroused considerable interest in the United States for a similar monument. Negotiations went on for more than two years before it was agreed that the obelisk standing in Alexandria might be removed. The work was given over to Lieutenant Commander Henry H. Gorringe of the United States Navy. Even though many difficulties had to be faced, Gorringe successfully transferred and erected the obelisk. In a dignified monograph, *Egyptian Obelisks,* he recounted his adventures.

The problems began when an Italian consul in Alexandria claimed that the land on which the obelisk stood was his and prevented work from being done to remove it. Negotiations went on between the Italian and American consuls. It was only when the former was theatened with a claim for damages that he agreed to accept a settlement. Work began, but while clearance was taking place around the base of the obelisk, a creditor of the Egyptian government appealed to the International Court to prevent its continuation until his claim was settled. This caused further delay. Finally, an American flag was hoisted atop the obelisk, and with this indication that it was now officially the property of the United States, the work was resumed.

Gorringe's technical problems now were to remove and load the obelisk. First it was necessary to clear around the obelisk and to expose its foundations. During this work many antiquities were encountered, and the obelisk proved to be standing on a pedestal atop a stepped foundation. Under the corners of the obelisk there had once been four bronze crabs, like those of the obelisk of the Piazza di Sân Pietro in Rome, but in Alexandria only two remained. (These are now in the Metropolitan Mu-

PLATE 47. Latin inscription on one of the bronze crabs from the base of the New York obelisk

seum of Art, New York.) On each of the crabs was carved in both Greek and Latin the facts of the obelisk's erection in Alexandria: "In the eighteenth year of [Augustus] Caesar, [P. Rubrius] Barbarus, Prefect of Egypt, erected [it]; Pontius, architect" (plate 47).

Having cleared the site, Gorringe next had the delicate operation of bringing the obelisk down from its pedestal. In the presence of the governor of Alexandria and several hundred Egyptians and foreigners, it was successfully lowered and placed into a sort of caisson.

The pedestal and some of the underlying steps were removed, and the obelisk and its container were then transferred to the port. The only road which could be taken was a long and indirect one, but the journey was satisfactorily accomplished, albeit with great effort and great expense.

Negotiations had been going on for some time for the purchase of the ship *Dessug*, built in England for the Postal Department of the Egyptian government. At last a price was agreed upon, and alterations were made to strengthen the steamer so that it could carry the obelisk and its pedestal. At the port, the pedestal, which weighed about 50 tons, was lifted with a crane to the deck of the ship. To load the obelisk, it was necessary to put the steamer in dry dock. An opening was then made in the hull, and by means of two hydraulic jacks the obelisk was brought up to that level and pushed inside onto a wooden platform designed to keep it steady during the voyage.

At last, the obelisk was on board, and the steamer was ready to sail, but there was still a problem. It proved impossible to find in Alexandria any men who were willing to man the ship and make the voyage. After considerable time, a crew was finally enlisted in the city of Trieste at the head of the Adriatic Sea. After a delay of months, the *Dessug* began its journey to the New World. It was not an easy voyage; many accidents happened along the way, sometimes endangering the ship and ita cargo. Finally the ship anchored at the Quarantine Station in New York on July 20, 1880.

When the ship arrived, a site for the obelisk, although discussed for some time, had not yet been finally chosen. On July 27, the Board of Commissioners of the Department of Parks at last made its difficult decision: the obelisk was to be set up on the summit of Graywacke Knoll in Central Park.

The pedestal and its stepped foundation had first to be transferred to the site. There was no problem with the foundation, but the 50-ton pedestal presented difficulty. On August 4, this colossal stone was lifted out of the steamer and placed on the dock. It was then moved onto a truck and dragged through the streets of the city by thirty-two horses hitched in sixteen pairs. Gorringe wrote that "this stone is the largest and heaviest ever moved on wheels of which there is any record, and excepting the obelisk it is the largest ever moved through New York."

The foundation steps were laid down in Central Park just as they had been in Alexandria, although room was left among them for hermetically sealed lead boxes which were designed to hold foundation deposits. On October 9, 1880, in a ceremony presided over by the grand master of the Masons in the state of New York, the pedestal was set in place. On that day, some 9,000 Masons and not less than 30,000 other spectators witnessed the ceremonies.

Once the pedestal was in place, the task of getting the obelisk itself from the *Dessug* to Central Park remained. Many proposals were made as to where the obelisk could best be disembarked and by what route it should be taken to its destination. At last Staten Island was chosen for the disembarkation. With the help of the tide, the bow of the *Dessug* was hauled out of the water at Luxor's Marine Railway on the eastern shore of the island, and the obelisk was removed from the ship. It was placed on pontoons and towed across the bay to Manhattan, then it proceeded in stately fashion through the streets of the city, traveling at the rate of 29.5 meters a day. It made its journey of 3323.5 meters from the landing place to the site in Central Park in 112 days, arriving on January 5, 1881.

A little over two weeks later, the obelisk was raised amid the cheers of more than 10,000 spectators (plate 48). With this the formidable undertaking was at an end. Fifteen months had elapsed from the day the work of removal had begun in Alexandria. Only the formal presentation of the obelisk by the nation to the City of New York remained, and this took place on February 22 in the presence of many dignitaries and a crowd of 20,000.

The ceremony was marked by a long speech by William Maxwell Evarts, then U.S. secretary of state. In it, he thanked Egypt for this generous gift and applauded Gorringe for his feat of bringing the obelisk safely to the United States. Evarts also spoke of the Assyrian, Roman, and Byzantine empires: they too had taken obelisks from Egypt, and their great civilizations, like that of Egypt itself, had come to an end. What, he asked, would become of the civilizations of England, France, and the United States, which had so recently acquired obelisks?

PLATE 48. Erection of the New York obelisk in Central Park

PLATE 49
The top of the New York
obelisk, showing recent
effects of its current
environment

PLATE 50. The New York obelisk

"Who indeed can tell what our nation will do if any perversity is possible of realization; and yet this obelisk may ask us, 'Can you expect to flourish forever? Can you expect wealth to accumulate and man not decay? Can you think that the soft folds of luxury are to wrap themselves closer and closer around this nation and the pith and vigor of its manhood know no decay? Can it creep over you and yet the nation know no decrepitude? These are questions that may be answered in the time of the obelisk but not in ours." [24]

When the New York obelisk was set up, the city did not possess the modern skyscrapers for which it has become famous. Even now, isolated in the expanse of Central Park, the obelisk is not dwarfed by its colossal neighbors. Queen Hatshepsut wrote that the tops of her obelisks penetrated the sky, and Tuthmosis III claimed that his mingled with the sky. It is fitting that the oldest "skyscraper" in a city of skyscrapers should be one from ancient Egypt. What is to be deplored is the fact that this obelisk has deteriorated more than any other of these transplanted monuments from the environment of its new home (plate 49).

REFERENCE NOTES

CHRONOLOGICAL TABLES

SUGGESTIONS
FOR FURTHER READING

ILLUSTRATION CREDITS

INDEX

Reference Notes

LIST OF ABBREVIATIONS

ASAE: Annales du Service des Antiquités de l'Égypte, Cairo, 1900–.
JEA: Journal of Egyptian Archaeology, London, 1914–.
MDAIK: Mitteilungen des deutschen Instituts für ägyptische Altertumskunde in Kairo, Berlin, 1930–.
ZÄS: Zeitschrift für ägyptische Sprache und Altertumskunde, Leipzig and Berlin, 1863–.

I. THE MEANING OF OBELISKS

1. More detailed commentary upon the religious significance of obelisks and the deities associated with them may be found under the appropriate headings in Hans Bonnet, Reallexikon der ägyptischen Religionsgeschichte (Berlin: Walter de Gruyter, 1952).

2. Pyramid text § 1652; R. O. Faulkner, The Ancient Egyptian Pyramid Texts (Oxford: The Clarendon Press, 1969), p. 242.

3. Pliny the Elder, Natural History, 36.14.

4. Alexandre Moret, Le Rituel du culte divin journalier en Égypte (Paris: Ernest Leroux, 1902), p. 242.

5. Georges Daressy, "Graffiti de la Montagne Rouge," ASAE 13 (1914):43–7; the inscriptions accompanying the scene were made by the chief of works Penameny.

6. Christiane Desroches-Noblecourt, "À propos de l'obélisque de Saint-Jean-de-Latran et d'un sanctuaire en vogue à Karnak à la fin de la XVIIIe dynastie," ASAE 50 (1950):257–67.

7. Reginald Engelbach, "The Direction of the Inscriptions on Obelisks," ASAE 29 (1929):25–30.

8. Norman de Garis Davies, The Tomb of Rekh-mi-rē' at Thebes, 2 vols. (New York: Metropolitan Museum of Art, 1943):2, pl. 83.

9. Encyclopaedia Britannica, 1972 ed., "Obelisks."

II. HOW OBELISKS WERE PRODUCED

1. For a more technical study of these types of stone, see J. R. Harris, Lexicographical Studies in Ancient Egyptian Minerals (Berlin: Akademie-Verlag, 1961), pp. 72–74.

2. The discussion of obelisks in this chapter follows Reginald Engelbach, *The Problem of the Obelisks* (New York: George H. Doran, 1923), pp. 21–22.

3. Ibid., pp. 41–42.

4. Ibid., p. 44.

5. Ibid., pp. 48–49.

6. Personal communication to the author.

7. Engelbach, *Problem of the Obelisks*, p. 54.

8. For a recent discussion of the problems involved in moving obelisks, see Henri Chevrier, "Technique de la construction dans l'ancienne Égypte. II. Problèmes posés par les obélisques." *Revue d'Égyptologie* 22 (1970):15–39.

9. Edouard Naville, *The Temple of Deir el-Bahari*, 6, Excavation Memoir 29 (London: Egypt Exploration Fund, 1908), pp. 2–6, pls. 103–106.

10. Engelbach, *Problem of the Obelisks*, pp. 69–70.

11. Henri Chevrier, "Note sur l'érection des obélisques," *ASAE* 52 (1954):309–313.

12. Henri Chevrier, "Rapport sur les travaux de Karnak: Colonne de Taharqa," *ASAE* 29 (1929):134–135, pl. 1.

13. William Mathew Flinders Petrie, *Arts and Crafts of Ancient Egypt* (Chicago: A. C. McClurg, 1910), p. 72.

14. Pierre Lacau, "L'Or dans l'architecture égyptienne," *ASAE* 53 (1956):221–250; especially 241–247.

15. Anastasi, I, 14.2–17.2; Alan H. Gardiner, *Egyptian Hieratic Texts* (Leipzig: J. C. Hinrichs'sche Buchhanlung, 1911), pp. 31*–34*.

16. Herodotus, *Histories*, 2.175.

17. Pliny the Elder, *Natural History*, 36.14.

18. Engelbach, *Problem of the Obelisks*, p. 91.

III. HELIOPOLIS AND MEMPHIS

1. My translation of Roger Godel, *Platon a Héliopolis d'Égypte* (Paris: Société d'édition "Les belles lettres," 1956), p. 16.

2. Labib Habachi, "Hekaib, the Deified Governor of Elephantine," *Archeology* 9 (1956):9–15.

3. Personal communication to the author.

4. For a recent translation of the story, see William Kelly Simpson, ed., *The Literature of Ancient Egypt* (New Haven, Conn.: Yale University Press, 1972), pp. 15–30.

5. This type of temple is described in detail by Jacques Vandier, *Manuel d'archéologie égyptienne* 2 (Paris: Éditions A. et J. Picard, 1955), pp. 582–594.

6. For all these obelisks, see Charles Kuentz, *Obélisques*, Catalogue Général des Antiquités Egyptiennes du Musée du Caire (Cairo: Institut Français d'Archéologie Orientale, 1932), p. 1 ff.

7. Adrian de Buck, "The Building Inscription of the Berlin Leather Roll," *Studia Aegyptiaca* I (Rome: Pontificium Institutum Biblicum, 1938), pp. 48–57.

8. Herbert Ricke, "Eine Inventartafel aus Heliopolis im Turiner Museum," *ZAS* 71 (1935):111–133, pls. 2–3.

9. As quoted in E. A. Wallis Budge, *Cleopatra's Needles and Other Egyptian Obelisks* (London: The Religious Tract Society, 1926), pp. 84–86.

10. Ibid., pp. 85–86.

11. W. M. Flinders Petrie and Ernest Mackay, *Heliopolis, Kafr Ammar and Shurafa* (London: School of Archaeology in Egypt and Bernard Quaritch, 1915), pp. 5–6, pls. 4–5.

IV. THEBES AND OTHER CITIES

1. Ammianus Marcellinus, 17.6–8, as quoted in Budge, *Cleopatra's Needles*, p. xxiv.

2. Homer, *Iliad*, 9.382–385.

3. James Henry Breasted, *Ancient Records of Egypt*, 5 vols. (Chicago: University of Chicago Press, 1906), 2. 40–44.

4. Compare Breasted, *Ancient Records*, 2. 147.

5. Labib Habachi, "Two Graffiti at Sehēl from the Reign of Queen Hatshepsut," *Journal of Near Eastern Studies* 16 (1957):88–104, pls. 16, 17.

6. Ibid., p. 92.

7. Marquis of Northhampton et al., *Report on some Excavations in the Theban Necropolis during the Winter of 1898–9* (London: Archibald Constable and Co. Ltd., 1908), pp. 15–17, pl. 1.

8. Norman de Garis Davies, *The Tomb of Puyemre at Thebes*, 2 vols (New York: Metropolitan Museum of Art, 1922), 1. 97–98, pls. 37–39.

9. William C. Hayes believes that these represented obelisks erected in Thebes for the second and third Jubilees and in Heliopolis for the fourth Jubilee. See "A Statute of the Herald Yamu-Nedjeh in the Egyptian Museum, Cairo, and Some Biographical Notes on its Owner," *ASAE* 33 (1933):6–16, plate, and Erik Iversen, *Obelisks in Exile*, 2 (Copenhagen, G. E. C. Gad., 1972), pl. II, pp. 145, 146.

10. Nina M. de Garis Davies and Norman de Garis Davies, *The Tombs of Menkheperrasonb, Amenmose and Another (Nos. 86, 112, 42, 226)* (London: Egypt Exploration Society, 1933), pl. 10 and p. 11 ff.

11. Engelbach, *Problem of the Obelisks*, p. 27.

12. Labib Habachi, "Notes on the Unfinished Obelisk of Aswân and Another Smaller One in Gharb Aswân." *Drevniā Egipet, Sbornik Stateiā* (Moscow: Akademii Nauk SSSR, 1960), pp. 216–235.

13. For the obelisks of Amenophis II and Tuthmosis IV, see Kuentz, *Obélisques*, p. 30 ff.

14. Labib Habachi, "An Inscription at Aswān Referring to Six Obelisks," *JEA* 36 (1950):13–18, pl. 3.

15. Norman de Garis Davies, *The Tomb of Nefer-Hotep at Thebes*, 2 vols (New York: Metropolitan Museum of Art, 1933), 1. 28–32, pl. 41.

16. Desroches-Noblecourt, "L'Obélisque de Saint-Jean-de-Latran," in *ASAE*, 50(1950), pp. 257–267.

17. Kuentz, *Obélisques*, p. 34 ff.

V. PIRAMESSE AND OTHER CITIES

1. Ricardo A. Caminos, *Late-Egyptian Miscellanies* (London: Oxford University Press, 1954), pp. 73–75.

2. Compare Alan H. Gardiner, "Tanis and Pi-Ramesse: A Retraction," *JEA* 19 (1933):122–128.

3. Labib Habachi, "Khatâ'na-Qantîr: Importance," *ASAE* 52 (1954):443–562, pls. 1–37.

4. Labib Habachi, "The Two Rock-Stelae of Sethos I in the Cataract Area Speaking of Huge Statues and Obelisks," *Bulletin de l'Institut français d'archéologie orientale* 73 (1973):113–125, pls. 10–11.

5. Habachi, "Notes on the Unfinished Obelisk of Aswan," pp. 224–235.

6. Alexander Badawy, "A Monumental Gateway for a Temple of Sety I: An Ancient Model Restored," *Miscellanea Wilbouriana* 1 (1972):1–23, cf. 15, frontispiece.

7. Siegfried Schott, "Zwei Obeliskensockel aus Athribis," *MDAIK* 8 (1939):190–197.

8. Pierre Montet, "Les Obélisques de Ramses II," *Kêmi* 5 (1935–37): 104–114, pls. 1–34; (2nd article) by T. Ledant and T. Yoyotte, *Kêmi* 11 (1950): 73–84, pls. 8–9; (3rd article) by T. Ledant and T. Yoyotte, *Kêmi* 14 (1957):43–80. For this obelisk see vol. 5, p. 109 ff. and pl. 14.

9. A comprehensive listing of the published accounts of the building projects of Ramesses II at the Temple of Luxor appears in Bertha Porter and Rosalind L. B. Moss, *Topographical Bibliography of Ancient Egyptian Hieroglyphic Texts, Reliefs, and Paintings, 2, Theban Temples*, 2d ed. (Oxford: At the Clarendon Press, 1972), pp. 302–312, especially 302 ff.

10. Breasted, *Ancient Records*, 3, 234–237.

11. Paul Barguet, *Le Temple d'Amon-Rè à Karnak* (Cariro: Institut français d'archeologie orientale, 1962), p. 223.

12. Kuentz, "Obélisques," p. 53 ff.

13. Ibid., p. 59 ff.

14. Ibid., p. 62 ff.

15. Ibid., p. 61 ff.

16. Günther Roeder, "Vorläufiger Bericht über die Deutsche Hermopolis-Expedition 1938 und 1939," *MDAIK* 9 (1940): pl. 12b.

17. Kuentz, *Obélisques,* p. 66 ff.

18. Badge, *Cleopatra's Needles,* pp. 230–243.

VI. ROME AND ISTANBUL

1. The account of the obelisks of Rome follows that given by Erik Iversen, *Obelisks in Exile: The Obelisks of Rome* (Copenhagen: G. E. C. Gad, 1968); and that by Cesare D'Onofrio, *Gli Obelischi di Roma,* 2nd ed. (Rome: Bulzoni, 1967).

2. Gustavo Lefebvre, "Sur l'obélisque du Latran," *Mélanges d'archéologie et d'historie offerts à Charles Picard* (Paris: Presses universitaires de France, 1949), pp. 586–593.

3. Paul Barguet, "L'Obélisque de Saint-Jean-de-Latran dans le temple de Ramsès II à Karnak," *ASAE* 50 (1950):269–280.

4. Hans Wolfgang Müller, "Der Obelisk von Urbino," *ZAS* 79 (1954):143–149, pl. 15.

5. Iversen, *Obelisks in Exile,* 1. p. 16.

6. Ibid., p. 128.

7. Ibid., p. 81.

8. The history of the Istanbul obelisk is recorded in Gerda Bruns, *Der Obelisk und seine Basis auf dem Hippodrom zu Konstantinopel* (Istanbul: Universum-Druckerei, 1935).

9. Ibid., fig. 13, p. 16.

VII. PARIS, LONDON, AND NEW YORK

1. The account of the transport of the Paris obelisk follows the version in Jean Baptiste Apollinaire Lébas, *L'Obélisque de Luxor* (Paris: Carilian-Goeury et Vr. Dalmont, 1839).

2. As quoted in Aubrey Noakes, *Cleopatra's Needles* (London: H. F. & G. Witherby, 1962), p. 1.

3. My translation of Lébas, *Obélisque,* p. 28.

4. Ibid., pp. 28–29.

5. Ibid., p. 41.

6. Ibid., p. 45.

7. Ibid.

8. Ibid., p. 69.

9. Ibid., p. 89.

10. Ibid., p. 90.

11. Ibid., p. 148.

12. Leslie Greener, *The Discovery of Egypt* (New York: Viking, 1967), p. 160.

13. James Henry Breasted, "The Obelisk of Thutmose III and His Building Season in Egypt," *ZAS* 39 (1901):55.

14. The story of the removal of the London obelisk follows that given by Noakes, *Cleopatra's Needles*.

15. Ibid., p. 16.

16. Ibid., p. 20.

17. Ibid.

18. Ibid., p. 24.

19. Iversen, *Obelisks in Exile: The Obelisks of Istanbul and England* (Copenhagen: G.E.C. Gad., 1972)2. p. 118.

20. Noakes, *Cleopatra's Needles,* p. 46.

21. Ibid., p. 91.

22. Ibid.

23. The account of the removal of the New York obelisk follows that given by Henry H. Gorringe, *Egyptian Obelisks* (New York: published by the author, 1882).

24. Ibid., p. 53.

Chronological Tables

1. THE MAJOR PERIODS OF EGYPTIAN HISTORY, INCLUDING THE NAMES OF INDIVIDUAL RULERS ASSOCIATED WITH OBELISKS

SOURCES

The Cambridge Ancient History, 3rd ed., vols. I and II (Cambridge: At the University Press, 1970–1975), and Sir Alan Gardiner, *Egypt of the Pharaohs* (Oxford: the Clarendon Press, 1961).

Archaic Period, Dynasties I–II (c.3100–2686)
  First Dynasty (c.3100–2890)
Old Kingdom, Dynasties III–VI (2686–2181)
  Fourth Dynasty (2613–2498)
    Cheops 2591–2566
  Fifth Dynasty (2494–2345)
    Neuserre (2450–2420)
  Sixth Dynasty (2345–2181)
    Teti 2345–2333
    Pepi I 2333–2385
    Pepi II 2269–2185
First Intermediate Period, Dynasties VII–mid-XI (2181–2050)
Middle Kingdom, Dynasties mid-XI–XII (2050–1786)
  Twelfth Dynasty (1991–1786)
    Sesostris I 1971–1928
Second Intermediate Period, Dynasties XIII–XVII (1786–1570)
  Seventeenth Dynasty (1650–1570)
    Nubkheperre Antef after 1600
New Kingdom, Dynasties XVIII–XX (1570–1085)
  Eighteenth Dynasty (1570–1320)
    Ahmose 1570–1546
    Amenophis I 1546–1526

Tuthmosis I 1525–c. 1512.
Tuthmosis II c.1512–1504
Tuthmosis III 1504–1450
Hatshepsut 1503–1482
Amenophis II 1450–1425
Tuthmosis IV 1425–1417
Amenophis III 1417–1379
Akhenaten 1379–1362
Smenkhkare 1364–1361
Tutankhamen 1361–1352
Ay 1352–1348
Haremhab 1348–1320
Nineteenth Dynasty, "Ramesside" (1320–1200)
  Ramesses I 1320–1318
  Sethos I 1318–1304
  Ramesses II 1304–1237
  Merneptah 1236–1223
  Sethos II 1216–1210
Twentieth Dynasty, "Ramesside" (1200–1085)
  Ramesses IV 1166–1160
  Ramesses VI 1156–1148
Third Intermediate Period, Dynasties XXI–XXV (1085–665)
  Twenty-first Dynasty (1085–945)
  Twenty-second and Twenty-third Dynasties (945–730)

Twenty-fourth Dynasty (720–715)
Twenty-fifth Dynasty, "Ethiopian" (715–656)
  Taharka 689–664
Saite Period, Dynasty XXVI (664–525)
  Psammetikos II 595–589
  Apries 589–570
  Amasis 570–526
Late Period, Dynasties XXVII–XXX (524–343)

Twenty-seventh Dynasty, "Persian" (525–404)
Twenty-eighth Dynasty (404–399)
Twenty-ninth Dynasty (399–380)
Thirtieth Dynasty (380–343)
  Nectanebo II 360–343
Ptolemaic Period (323–30)
  Ptolemy II 285–246
  Ptolemy IX 116–81

2. ROMAN EMPERORS CONCERNED WITH OBELISKS

Augustus 27 B.C.–A.D. 14
Tiberius A.D. 14–37
Caligula (Gaius) 37–41
Vespasian 69–79
Titus 79–81
Domitian 81–96
Hadrian 117–138

Commodus 180–192
Gallienus 253–268
Maxentius 306–312
Constantine 306–337
Constantius 337–361
Julian 361–363
Theodosius 379–395

3. POPES CONCERNED WITH OBELISKS

Gregory XIII 1572–1585
Sixtus V 1585–1590
Innocent X 1644–1655
Alexander VII 1655–1667
Clement XI 1700–1721

Clement XII 1730–1740
Benedict XIV 1740–1758
Clement XIV 1769–1772
Pius VI 1772–1799
Pius VII 1800–1823

Suggestions for Further Reading

The following are some of the major works dealing with obelisks:

Bonnet, Hans. *Reallexikon der Ägyptischen Religionsgeschichte*. Berlin: Walter de Gruyter, 1952.

Bruns, Gerda. *Der Obelisk und seine Basis auf dem Hippodrom zu Konstantinopel*. Istanbul: Universum-Druckerei, 1935.

Budge, E. A. Wallis. *Cleopatra's Needles and Other Egyptian Obelisks*. London: Religious Tract Society, 1926.

Byvanck, Alexander Willem. *De Obelisk van Constantinopel*. Amsterdam: Noord-Hollandsche Uitg., 1960.

Cooper, William R. *A Short History of the Egyptian Obelisks*. London: S. Bagster and Sons, 1877.

Dibner, Bern. *Moving the Obelisks*. Cambridge, Mass.: M.I.T. Press, 1970.

Engelbach, Reginald. *The Aswan Obelisk*, Cairo: Institut français d'archéologie orientale, 1922.

———. The Problem of the Obelisks. New York: George H. Doran, 1923.

Gorringe, Henry H. *Egyptian Obelisks*. New York: published by the author, 1882.

Iversen, Erik. *Obelisks in Exile*. Copenhagen: G. E. C. Gad. 1. *The Obelisks of Rome*, 1968. 2. *The Obelisks of Istanbul and England*, 1972. 3. *The Obelisks of Italy, Germany, France and the United States*, in preparation.

Kastl, Helmut, and Olaf Hein. *Gli Obelischi di Roma e le loro epigrafi*. Rome: Edizione d'Italia, 1970.

Kuentz, Charles. *Obélisques*, Catalogue général des antiquités égyptiennes du Musée du Caire. Cairo: Institut Français d'Archéologie Orientale, 1932.

Lébas, Jean Baptiste Apollinaire. *L'Obélisque de Luxor*. Paris: Carilian-Goeury et Vr. Dalmont, 1839.

Marucchi, Orazio. *Gli Obelischi egiziani di Roma*. Rome: E. Looscher, 1868.

Moldenke, Charles E. *The New York Obelisk, Cleopatra's Needle*. New York: A. D. F. Randolph.

Noakes, Aubrey. *Cleopatra's Needles*. London: H. F. & G. Witherby Ltd., 1962.

Onofrio, Cesare d'. *Gli Obelischi di Roma*. 2nd ed. Rome: Bulzoni, 1967.

Rühlmann, Gerhard. *Die Nadeln des Pharao*. Dresden: VEB Verlag der Kunst, 1968.

Illustration Credits

Index